OUTCOMES OF ENGAGED EDUCATION: FROM TRANSFER TO TRANSFORMATION

PRACTICES & POSSIBILITIES

Series Editors: Aimee McClure, Kelly Ritter, Aleashia Walton, and Jagadish Paudel

Consulting Editor: Mike Palmquist

The Practices & Possibilities Series addresses the full range of practices within the field of Writing Studies, including teaching, learning, research, and theory. From Richard E. Young's taxonomy of "small genres" to Patricia Freitag Ericsson's edited collection on sexual harassment in the academy to Jessie Borgman and Casey McArdle's considerations of teaching online, the books in this series explore issues and ideas of interest to writers, teachers, researchers, and theorists who share an interest in improving existing practices and exploring new possibilities. The series includes both original and republished books. Works in the series are organized topically.

The WAC Clearinghouse and University Press of Colorado are collaborating so that these books will be widely available through free digital distribution and low-cost print editions. The publishers and the series editors are committed to the principle that knowledge should freely circulate and have embraced the use of technology to support open access to scholarly work.

OTHER BOOKS IN THE SERIES

Charles Bazerman, *Unfinished Business: Thoughts on the Past, Present, Future, and Nurturing of Homo Scribens* (2024)

E. Shelley Reid, *Rethinking Your Writing: Rhetoric for Reflective Writers* (2024)

Asao B. Inoue and Kristin DeMint Bailey (Eds.), *Narratives of Joy and Failure in Antiracist Assessment: Exploring Collaborative Writing Assessments* (2024)

Asao B. Inoue, *Cripping Labor-Based Grading for More Equity in Literacy Courses* (2023)

Jessie Borgman and Casey McArdle (Eds.), *PARS in Charge: Resources and Strategies for Online Writing Program Leaders* (2023)

Douglas Hesse and Laura Julier (Eds.), *Nonfiction, the Teaching of Writing, and the Influence of Richard Lloyd-Jones* (2023)

Linda Adler-Kassner and Elizabeth Wardle, *Writing Expertise: A Research-Based Approach to Writing and Learning Across Disciplines* (2022)

Michael J. Faris, Courtney S. Danforth, and Kyle D. Stedman (Eds.), *Amplifying Soundwriting Pedagogies: Integrating Sound into Rhetoric and Writing* (2022)

Crystal VanKooten and Victor Del Hierro (Eds.), *Methods and Methodologies for Research in Digital Writing and Rhetoric: Centering Positionality in Computers and Writing Scholarship, Volumes 1 and 2* (2022)

OUTCOMES OF ENGAGED EDUCATION: FROM TRANSFER TO TRANSFORMATION

By Linda Flower

The WAC Clearinghouse
wac.colostate.edu
Fort Collins, Colorado

University Press of Colorado
upcolorado.com
Denver, Colorado

The WAC Clearinghouse, Fort Collins, Colorado 80523

University Press of Colorado, Denver, Colorado 80203

© 2024 by Linda Flower. This work is released under a Creative Commons Attribution-NonCommercial-NoDerivatives 4.0 International license.

ISBN 978-1-64215-238-8 (PDF) | 978-1-64215-239-5 (ePub) | 978-1-64642-688-1 (pbk.)

DOI 10.37514/PRA-B.2024.2388

Library of Congress Cataloging-in-Publication Data

Names: Flower, Linda, author.
Title: Outcomes of engaged education : from transfer to transformation / by Linda Flower.
Description: Fort Collins, Colorado : The WAC Clearinghouse ; Denver, Colorado : University Press of Colorado, 2024. | Series: Practices & possibilities | Includes bibliographical references and index.
Identifiers: LCCN 2024038722 (print) | LCCN 2024038723 (ebook) | ISBN 9781646426881 (paperback) | ISBN 9781642152388 (adobe pdf) | ISBN 9781642152395 (epub)
Subjects: LCSH: Community and college—United States. | College-school cooperation—United States. | Experiential learning—United States. | Educational evaluation—United States.
Classification: LCC LC238 .F59 2024 (print) | LCC LC238 (ebook) | DDC 378.1/03—dc23/eng/20240925
LC record available at https://lccn.loc.gov/2024038722
LC ebook record available at https://lccn.loc.gov/2024038723

Copyeditor: Don Donahue
Designer: Mike Palmquist
Cover Image: RawPixel Image 5948414. Licensed
Series Editors: Aimee McClure, Kelly Ritter, Aleashia Walton, and Jagadish Paudel
Consulting Editor: Mike Palmquist

The WAC Clearinghouse supports teachers of writing across the disciplines. Hosted by Colorado State University, it brings together scholarly journals and book series as well as resources for teachers who use writing in their courses. This book is available in digital formats for free download at wac.colostate.edu.

Founded in 1965, the University Press of Colorado is a nonprofit cooperative publishing enterprise supported, in part, by Adams State University, Colorado School of Mines, Colorado State University, Fort Lewis College, Metropolitan State University of Denver, University of Alaska Fairbanks, University of Colorado, University of Denver, University of Northern Colorado, University of Wyoming, Utah State University, and Western Colorado University. For more information, visit upcolorado.com.

Citation Information: Flower, Linda. (2024). *Outcomes of Engaged Education: From Transfer to Transformation*. The WAC Clearinghouse; University Press of Colorado. https://doi.org/1010.37514/PRA-B.2024.2388

Land Acknowledgment. The Colorado State University Land Acknowledgment can be found at landacknowledgment.colostate.edu.

Contents

Acknowledgments vii

Introduction 3

Chapter 1. Why Should Assessment Matter? 11

Chapter 2. Creating Personal Outcomes 29

Chapter 3. Outcomes with a Public Face 47

Chapter 4. Interrogating Hidden Frames as a Path to Change 69

Chapter 5. Putting Transformation to Work 93

Chapter 6. Teaching for Transformation 115

Works Cited 133

Index 143

Acknowledgments

This book is the work of many hands and hearts, starting with all those college students who have listened to, encouraged and mentored teenagers in Pittsburgh's urban Community Literacy Center, in Decision Makers on campus, and those who have drawn members of our local communities into collaborative Think Tanks. Their gift to us comes in the written reflections and interviews in which they gave serious thought to that experience in order to articulate what they made of it and how it then played a role—of many different sorts—in their own lives. At the same time these classes and projects have given me over the last twenty some years a set of colleagues, fellow researchers, and beloved friends that I can never thank enough. In its early years the style of community engagement sketched here took shape in written and in-person conversations with colleagues, the likes of Eli Goldblatt, Ellen Cushman, Steve Parks, Paula Mathieu, David Coogan—as we supported, challenged, and learned from each other's practice. The bibliography is my larger thank-you note.

For me, it all started with Wayne Peck, Elenore Long, and Lorraine Higgins who brought the Community Literacy Center vision to life and whose own writing has been a gift to our field. And to Mrs. Joyce Baskins for her laughing, wise and loving support to all of us. Wayne as director of the Community House brought not only his vision, but an on-the-ground ability to bring it to life. Lorraine not only invented the CLC's Argue project, but even took on the job of center director. Elenore' gift for listening shaped our approach to mentoring, which blossomed into the theory and practice of a "responsive rhetorical art" in her research and leadership. This collaboration and my colleagues' sense of adventure, imagination, caring and social commitment was the wellspring for the best we accomplished. (As CMU's founder, Andrew Carnegie, put it in 1900, "My heart is in the work.")

This work has been supported at various times by the OERI (Office of Educational Research and Improvement) through National Center for the Study of Writing at Berkeley and Carnegie Mellon and my colleagues Sarah Freedman and Glynda Hull. My happy collaboration with John R. (Dick) Hayes in cognitive psychology laid the foundation for what I brought from cognitive rhetoric and problem-solving to the CLC agenda. And from the beginning Pittsburgh's Howard Heinz and Grable Foundations, and Carnegie Mellon supported both our research and what were often unusual projects.

Over these years many students have not only contributed to this work, but have helped shape/reshape its vision and practices. To name just a few, I would thank Alex Helberg, Craig Moreau, Julia Bennett, Jimmy Lizama, Cody Januszko, Maggie Goss, Ryan Roderick, Maureen Mathison, Ryan Mitchell, Emily Dejeu Tim Dawson, Justin Mando, Lindsey Wotanis, Alyssa Fogel, Susan Swan, Maria Poznahovska, Jessica Heathcote, Elizabeth Wolff, and Ann Blakeslee. Christopher Brown, Audrey Strohm, Ana Cooke, Brad Walker, and Leslie Setlock.

On the journey the book itself took, I have had the most generous, insightful, and delightful group of traveling companions I could have ever wished for. The imprint of fresh ideas and personal support from Doug Cloud, Amanda Berardi Tennant, Derek Handley, Carolyn Commer, and Mary Glavan is to be found across these pages. Elenore Long's own work and wonderful advice—though multiple versions of this manuscript—has been a guiding light to me. This MS reflects not only her thoughtful reading/re-reading but even more her insight into how we can build connections with others. And if such friendship is not enough, I guess she actually deserves some credit for sharing with me her offspring, Pascale Jarvis, who has been one of the best, most thoughtful MS editors I have had the pleasure to work with.

Heather Falconer, Associate Publisher at the WAC Clearinghouse seemed to answer all my questions, guide my next steps—and turn everything around overnight. Dan Donahue's copyediting had a great eye for detail. Mike Palmquist, Founding Editor and Publisher, lived up to his remarkable reputation as an inventor of new ways of publishing that has made work in education so widely available. And from the beginning, he seemed to know exactly what I wanted to do, set us on the path, and gave me the sort of encouragement that lighted the way. I am so happy to be working with this team.

OUTCOMES OF ENGAGED EDUCATION: FROM TRANSFER TO TRANSFORMATION

Introduction

How This Book Started

The stories, observations and arguments you will read here owe their inspiration to an early morning walk with Wayne Peck at a 1998 American Educational Research Association Conference in San Diego. Wayne had chosen to use his M.Div. from Harvard to pastor a small, interracial, progressive church in Pittsburgh's urban Northside as well as wrap up his PhD in rhetoric at Carnegie Mellon. At this point, I was engaged with equal enthusiasm in how to turn the research, my colleague in psychology Dick (John. R.) Hayes and I had named "cognitive rhetoric," into "teachable" heuristics—strategies that our "expert" writers were showing us but our "novices" didn't seem to know. I had made a start with a textbook on problem-solving strategies for writing.

However, in that cool early morning air in San Diego, Wayne Peck made a remark that opened up a whole new path in my life. As he said, "You know, for all your CMU students are learning, they will succeed anyway, with or without greater skill in writing. But for the black and white inner-city teenagers in my neighborhood, being able to communicate in more public ways might make all the difference."

Somehow, despite growing up in Kansas and small-town Iowa, I knew he was right. And somehow, by that fall, we had invented the Community Literacy Center, joined forces with Ms. Joyce Baskins (a recognized African American advocate and "mother of the neighborhood" in Pittsburgh's Northside), and created a college course in literacy that combined reading in theory, research and social action in order to mentor a group of urban teenage writers. And we all learned a lot. Each semester a Community Literacy Center project took on an issue those teenagers were facing, from risk and respect, to stress, to gangs, to finding jobs, to police, which they explored in their own publishable newsletter and then dramatized and presented in a public Community Conversation to engage the audience in discussing the issues these teenagers knew so well.

This story is a good example of what is now being called "co-creation." In a review of Aimée Knight's argument for this practice in her *Community is the Way*, Christopher Castillo sketches three guiding principles for community based partnerships: 1) focus on communities' strengths and assets, 2) prioritize co-creation of knowledge with partners, and 3) work towards change in the process of community work (153). This is how we also described it at the time:

> The design and staffing of the CLC reflects its intercultural agenda which invites people to cross boundaries of race, age, class, and gender. Along with the present authors, Joyce Baskins brings 20 years of community activism to her advocacy for

> African-American youth. Donald Tucker brings experience as a jazz musician and construction foreman to engaging inner-city youth in designing community development videos, Elenore Long, a post-doctoral fellow . . . brings her research on literacy and social action, . . . and Kevin McCartan brings know-how in grassroots community development and construction to CLC projects (Peck, Flower, and Higgins 221).

One of the distinctive features of this program was that although our teenage writers may not have been models of "success" at doing school, here they were taking literate action, writing about real, often unspoken challenges they faced in their neighborhoods. When they walked into the Center to talk and write, they were the undisputed "experts." And the mentors from my class, who were identified as "Supporters," were just that. What we "taught" were strategies drawn from our research for problem-solving and decision-making, not simply for planning and revising but what for turned out to be our three most powerful strategies for inquiry: getting at the "Story-Behind-The-Story," digging out "Rival Interpretations," and exploring "Options and Outcomes." Each writer's Supporter then encouraged, challenged and helped Writers think through how to turn their insights into an effective text. That is, how to make teachers, administrators, even police officers who came to the Community Conversations or read their newsletters see their world a little differently. (A measure of success I always treasured was the angry high school English teacher who came up to me at a Conversation, to accuse us of making her newly confident student "think he could write." Apparently, we had different standards.

As director of Pittsburgh's Community House, Wayne Peck brought a historical perspective to this work. Founded in 1916 at the height of the settlement house movement, with its classrooms, kitchens, offices, gym, and swimming pool, Community House was designed to be a "place of connection," to create a "light house of education" for urban neighborhoods" (Peck et al. 201). For him, "the CLC seeks to reinvent the settlement house vision of community and university interaction, but this time with attention centered on collaborative problem solving and the appreciation of multiple kinds of expertise" (203). His account of Mark captures this kind of engagement.

> A bright and resourceful teenager, who like many African-American males, finds little that interests him in school and is frequently suspended. . . . A fifteen-year-old at a crossroads. . . . In a recent CLC project, for example, Mark and ten other teens used writing to investigate the reasons for the increase in school suspension in the public schools. To present this "policy paper" Mark and his peers organized a "community conversation" with the mayor, the media, the school board president, principals, and community residents, in which Mark performed a rap

written from a teen's perspective and his peers interpreted it for the audience. As the culmination of their eight-week project, the teens also presented a newsletter, "Whassup with Suspension," which has since become required reading for teachers and students in Mark's high school. (199–200)

Over the next 20 years this start-up drew in undergrad and graduate students. As non-profits do it morphed into new projects and research in new cities led by folks like Elenore Long and Lorraine Higgins. Many of these are referenced in the discussion, but the cases here will draw on my own experience. My own learning curve, later as a director of the university's Center for Community Outreach but more importantly as an ordinary college professor, led to new courses and different projects with nursing aides, welfare recipients, and "at-risk" freshmen, on problems emerging in organizations, colleges, universities, unions, and high schools. In search of outcomes of engaged education, this book will draw on various kinds of data from this series of projects at the CLC and Carnegie Mellon University.

One of these projects, Decision Makers, was designed with an innovative high school program for juniors and seniors with a learning disability. Coming to the Carnegie Mellon campus computer lab, these "Scholars" created a personal *Journey Book* about their own good, bad, and future decisions, while their Supporters, in my course on Literacy: Educational Theory and Community Practice, helped draw out their Scholar's own insight and expertise. A Decision Makers computer program we designed embedded their now easily publishable writing within an online guide with prompts and questions based on the same strategies developed at the CLC. As an added bonus, it allowed us to collect an on-going body of pre/post data on the changes in their "Reflective Decision Making" discussed in Chapter 3.

A second set of projects created a series of Community Think Tanks, visited in Chapters 2, 3, and 5. Students in my seminar on Leadership, Dialogue and Change organized their Community Think Tank around a campus or community issue. Collecting alternative, and often competing, representations of the problem and of options and outcomes from a variety of stakeholders, they then created a Briefing Book sent to all participants. The booklet prepared them for the problem-solving dialogues in a series of Round Table discussions, the results of which the students documented, and published online (www.cmu.edu/thinktank, accessed 4 April 2024). (See Chapter 2, Figure 2.1)

So these chapters grew out of my experience over 25 years with the folks in the CLC, Decision Makers, and the Community Think Tanks. It was these people with whom I was privileged to work who provide the substance and the insights of this book. And it was thinking back over those events, stories, and data we had collected, that I was struck with the significance of *what they were doing* with what they learned. And this became my motivation to go back and ask, *what were the outcomes for them?* Doing so revealed not only distinctive examples of *transfer*, but remarkable instances of *transformation* in which former college students and community writers rewrote and adapted that experience into significantly personal outcomes. Yet at the same time it was striking how little our standard methods of assessment look beyond the college classroom (and sometime internships). In particular, how little we know about the life *outcomes* for the students who took part in *community engaged education*.

A Particular Model of Engagement

This story has its own niche in the robust culture and history of community engagement. Its model of engagement can start with faculty who, like myself may have multiple relations to community engagement, but who have also had the opportunity to teach college courses with high expectations for intellectual engagement with theory and research (in my case in rhetoric, inquiry, social justice, and public deliberation) with students who are equally eager to become Supporters, dealing with challenging problems, in relationships across difference in which the community "Partner" is the knowledge expert. That's a long sentence but those interconnections are what make this such a fertile ground for learning. Here the college student must deal with many of the issues raised in the historical path from service to educational engagement—issues that involve collaborative relationships, reciprocity, positionality, on the one hand, and various forms of action for social justice, on the other—always in the context of a unique and unpredictable setting where success is never guaranteed.

To be more explicit, this book will explore a particular form of *community engaged education*. As an *educational* practice for college students, it creates a dialogue in which academic research and theory is not only studied but then embedded and tested in a *community experience* raising the challenge of dealing with difference. In this context of intercultural *engagement* students draw on a conceptual framework, sketched above, designed to support rhetorical praxis through action and reflection. With the goal of developing *working knowledge* based on inquiry and metacognitive understanding, the educational *outcome* for these students lies in whether and how this knowledge is adapted and *applied* in their lives beyond the classroom and college.

Working out of this paradigm for community engaged education, my goals are

- To explore our potential to make an even stronger case for engaged education (given what has been called a "crisis in the humanities") by documenting its outcomes.
- To expand our understanding of transfer beyond the classroom to reveal the even more powerful acts of knowledge transformation we are seeing.
- And, finally to consider new methods for tracking, assessing and giving public presence to the outcomes of engaged education.

What Can This Book Offer?

Privileged for over 25 years with this sort of educational engagement, I found I had amassed a collection of varied revealing accounts of outcomes students have seen for themselves. Unlike attitude surveys, they were chiefly designed not only to improve my own classes, but as a concluding assignment that would draw my students into the reflective inquiry that can transform learning. Each chapter will then describe:

- A particular kind of outcome, illustrated with a case study from these documents,
- And a non-experimental, teacher-based method we can use with our students to track their transfer and transformations, and to document those outcomes,
- Ending with a brief account of what we observed in our particular contexts using that method.

The final chapter describes some heuristics for introducing a framework for reflection, knowing that reflection on one's own practice will open the door to personal agency and deeper learning. It then reviews some ways students can carry out this inquiry themselves. In the same spirit in which each chapter makes a distinction between a method and what we ourselves observed, I want to emphasize how these methods can be adapted to the wide range of situations and goals different teachers will have.

Table 1. Outcomes, Tools, and Lenses

Key Outcomes	Tools and Lenses for Tracking	Chapter
A Case for Engaged Education	Activity Analysis as a Social, Cultural, Cognitive Lens	Chapter 1
Creating Personal Outcomes	Critical Incident Interviews and Activity Analysis	Chapter 2
Building Public Facing Outcomes	Circulation, Conflict, and Framing as Conceptual Lenses, A Statistical + an Interpretive Lens	Chapter 3
Interrogating Hidden Frames as a Path to Change	Frame and Metacognitive Analysis, Grounded Theory Building,	Chapter 4
Putting Transformation to Work	Reflection and Metacognition as Paths to Working Theories and Action	Chapter 5
Teaching for Transformation	Adaptive Leadership, Activity Analysis, and Grounded-Theory Building	Chapter 6

Putting this Work in Context

The title of this book, Outcomes of Engaged Education, needs a bit of an explanation. From a historical perspective, those terms can call to mind the broad change in academic culture that has united both the institutional outreach and the curriculum of colleges and universities with different communities and their needs. Looking back, there was obviously the long tradition of volunteerism and community service that spawned "service-learning" more generally. But it wasn't until the 1980s that it became the subject of research and assessment in education and educational psychology. In Alan S. Waterman's detailed though dated review, these "experiential learning" and "community-service learning programs" were only lightly connected to a curriculum and were assessed in terms of simple results (increased school attendance or grades) and holistic measures of attitudes. In 1985 "public service" gained status and visibility when the four presidents of Brown, Stanford, Georgetown, and the Education Commission of the States co-founded the non-profit Campus Compact to showcase the good work their students were doing. (By 2000 it had 700 member campuses.) In 1984 Ernest Boyer's influential Carnegie Reports (written as President of the Carnegie Foundation) began proposing a new paradigm of scholarship that would integrate, communicate, and apply knowledge through professional service.

But the sea change relevant here came when the practice of "service" was rewritten into "community collaboration" or "engaged education" in the academic field of writing, rhetoric, and communication studies. In 1989, Pittsburgh's Community House and Carnegie Mellon founded the Community Literacy Center. (As far as we knew, this was the first use of the particular term "community literacy.") The year 2000 saw the first issue of *Reflections*, in which its opening review of the previous ten years, announced both the enormous popularity of service learning and the confusion over what actually was (Adler-Kassner 28).

In the same year, Tom Deans' ground-breaking study, *Writing Partnerships: Service-Learning in Composition*, defined the purview of this new academic field as writing for community, writing about community, and writing with community. In the same year, the Conference on College Composition and Communication named a new special session for it. Later in the fall of 2021 the first issue of the *Community Literacy Journal* appeared. The lead article in that first issue was on the CLC. It was also the focus of Dean's chapter on "writing with" (two of his three recommended sources also came from the CLC). Back in 1998 the WAC Clearinghouse had opened its doors as an on-line, open-access publishing collaborative with contributions from more than 200 scholars from six continents. Although WAC is a standard bearer for writing in multiple disciplines and technology, it now offers access to 4,240 resources on service learning, 3,230 on community literacy, and 2,120 on community engagement. Obviously, there will be overlap in these lists, but again they signal the growing breadth of interest in community related scholarship.

This new academic community began to call its work by various names, from community literacy and collaboration to self-publishing, to public pedagogy, to civic, social, and educational engagement among others. It had moved from university-initiated outreach, to local, individual initiatives with nonprofits, from collaboratively designed projects and programs to expanding networks of groups. Moreover, if we look at the first issues of those new journals, from their beginning the context, sites, scope and concerns of this movement ranged from writing in the context of the first-year college experience, public housing, and community-based technological literacy programs, to analyzing labor market connections, designing writing centers, and sustaining woman-centered programs. Now, 25 years later, we are entering an even more heightened level of political engagement and critique, focused on racism and discrimination, and calls to act for social justice.

From the beginning, the scope of the new model of community engagement was remarkably broad, followed over the last 25 years by a continued expansion of its public visibility, funding and academic significance. In WAC, the clearinghouse for writing across the disciplines, community-linked research turns up across its sites, from professional writing to nursing to technical communication. As Ann Blakeslee and her colleagues note in "A Story of a Writing-Based Resource—and a Call to Engage" even "technical communication has made tremendous strides in enacting a social justice agenda . . . [which is] accountable to our communities and their members" (42). By the time of Eli Goldbatt, Steve Parks, and David Jolliffe's landmark 2008 Imagining Community Literacy Symposium, we were being called to increasingly public action by models of social activism and community publishing such as Steve Parks and Eli Goldblatt's New City Writing and Steve Parks *New City Community Press* and David Coogan's 2006 work for social change through community action and later prison writing. Now in a quick look through our journals and conferences, community engagement is even more emphatically focused on social justice.

However, as we will discuss in Chapter 1, our understanding of educational outcomes and the practice of assessing them is still somewhat murky. Although it goes beyond the measurement of community members' competency in reading and writing that dominated early outreach programs, the assessment of their college mentors is largely dependent on broad holistic evaluation and attitude assessments. For example, a recent study using multiple sophisticated research methods, is giving us an expanded view of the broad outcomes of community-based engagement for college students. They conclude it "has been connected to increases in civic attitudes and civic mindedness; civic and community engagement, including increased value of engaging with the community" which includes feeling both the value of engagement and its social responsibility and obligation (Chittum et al. 16). However, they point out, although the research has expanded, "higher education still has much to learn about the efficacy of community-based experiences" (16).

We have work to do.

Chapter 1. Why Should Assessment Matter?

Walking across campus to my office, I pass the well-endowed computer science complex and the new fine arts building. On the sidewalk, red inlays display the names of faculty and students in the performing arts who have taken home Emmy, Oscar, Grammy, and Tony awards over the years. The lampposts that line the sidewalk are likewise decorated with banners celebrating the accomplishments of my colleagues with photos of them in their labs, where they test a robot or write calculations on the board. The banner titles herald these faculty as "The Innovators." As you might guess, the award winners are primarily in science, engineering, information systems, or the high-profile performing arts. A recent email from our new president celebrated a leadership appointment in Marketing and Communications that will "highlight our breadth and depth in scholarship, education and *societal impact*" (emphasis added).

All these symbolic messages illustrate the value we place on visible outcomes that have equally visible social impact. A more familiar parallel message in our own field, journals, and departments, however, is likely to note that the liberal arts are in crisis—or to be more precise, face being rendered obsolete, irrelevant to new realities, and underfunded in an age of austerity. And it raises the question: How do we point out our visible outcomes and societal impact? I hear John Dewey insisting that the meaning and worth of the ideas and practices we teach reside in the consequences of holding those ideas. And in the outcomes.

Socially Engaged Education

Our field, especially the committed educators referenced here, has long been working to make a case for many sorts of community engagement. Appearing in rhetoric, communication, composition, and English journals, the proposed responses to the question of our worth can range from assertively defending the scholarly status quo to instead calling us to engage with a public on its own terms around its felt dilemmas. The particular focus of my contribution here will be on a form of engagement that ties the serious study of rhetoric and learning to locally-engaged action—a kind of learning not defined by the acquisition of familiar bodies of knowledge, but by the construction and use of productive knowledge that is measured by outcomes. And a focus, in particular, on a still rare form of assessment based on actual outcomes for the engaged college student.

This chapter starts by sketching a particular paradigm of community-based socially engaged learning emerging in rhetorical studies and educational research: a paradigm in which an explicit goal of education is both judgment and wise action (based on what rhetoric describes as *phronésis*, or practical wisdom). Here the product of learning includes situated knowledge, and evaluation is based on the test of transfer beyond the classroom. Within this paradigm, we begin to see the unique educational value of courses that can draw students into a purposeful engagement with public issues, community interests, exigencies, and people. When students begin to take this engaged stance toward their own learning, they move toward the goals Linda Adler-Kassner and Peggy O'Neill set for the field: "We . . . must learn how to communicate our knowledge effectively beyond our own discipline and specialties so we can affect the discussions being held in state legislatures, departments of education, corporate boards, public commissions, and public forums" (qtd. in Welch 703). Such learning, I would add, also includes how to listen for and understand those needs.

In her excellent analysis of the public turn in composition, Ashley Holmes shows why it has emerged as such a powerful model of community engagement. *Public Pedagogy in Composition Studies* lays out a probing introduction to Henry Giroux and his "critical analysis" of the neo-liberal logic of our culture that promotes consumerism and individualism. In response, Holmes' case study research shows us ways "public pedagogy" can also allow students to enter and "engage public spaces as a method of analysis and critique" (13). The "spatial shock" of entering those spaces can not only reveal social-produced assumptions but trigger reflection on our own positionality (25). Nevertheless, as Phyllis Ryder argues, "the university [also] operates in a space saturated with neoliberal justifications for its purpose: to boost the economy, to create good workers, and to create its 'products' efficiently" (qtd. in Holmes 16–17). Recognizing that the problem is not just "out there," is one reason the notion of "location" and the "relocation" of the classroom has gained prominence. As John Ackerman and David Coogan's *The Public Work of Rhetoric* makes explicit, that work "is not shaped in our treatises and classrooms alone but in the material and discursive histories of communities outside of academe" (1–2).

Nevertheless, giving social significance a central place in a liberal curriculum will face two hurdles. First, if we attend to Dewey's insistence that the meaning of an idea resides in the consequences of holding that idea, then we must be able to articulate and show *what* those consequences are. How do we understand, much less track, those outcomes in which learning is measured not by tests and papers, but by rhetorical *praxis*: socially situated inquiry, dialogue, reflection and action?

Second, to complicate this agenda, a focus on outcomes has taken on a new, politically loaded meaning in contemporary education. "Outcomes" has been appropriated as the God-word of a neoliberal agenda designed to produce (and selectively subsidize) quantifiable, marketable skills as defined by the corporate sector and the ever-growing educational assessment industry.[1]

---

1. To put this market-based approach to education in a historical context, Carolyn Commer's gripping study of the controversy raised by the 2005 Spellings Commission report tracks the heated reception of the Department of Education's attempt to increase "accountability" in higher education. The red flag that aroused educators was not only this

Nancy Welch and Tony Scott's edited collection *Composition in the Age of Austerity* offers us competing arguments for how our field should respond to this "felt sense of crisis... in writing education" (4). In a review of those essays, David Grant notes how some of the most vigorous critiques reveal the engine of neoliberalism at work, actively shaping "how policy has changed to reward outcomes rather than inputs, where the educational emphasis on outcomes is typically placed in opposition to 'experience'" (12). To be more specific, experience is a valued outcome in a neoliberal education when it is transferrable to a marketable *work* experience. And those institutional forces that control cuts in funding, staff, and courses devalue any effort to create a traditional, if somewhat unspecified, "broadening experience" by asking instead for indicators of success that can be measured by assessment. So here's the rub: The assessment these institutions have in mind is based on functionalist measures associated with the neoliberal premise Scott describes as "the embedded commonsense principle that most spheres of human life are better perceived, managed, and evaluated as markets" (qtd. in Grant 8).

Fortunately, that is not the only way to play this game. Deborah Mutnick's response to austerity calls us to "address these problems through on-going work ... [that can] reclaim assessment and perform it on our own terms" (qtd. in Welch and Scott 40). I think of this as a call for grounded-theory building in which we must create both an expanded image of what we are after (an expanded theory of knowledge) and the methods to recognize it. This image, philosopher Sandra Harvey argues, makes a difference: it "answers questions about who can be a 'knower' ... what tests beliefs must pass in order to be legitimated as knowledge ... [and] what kinds of things can be known" (qtd. in Shah 14). Imagine, for example, an expanded image of knowledge, its knowers and its tests that might recognize the standing of local, rural, impoverished or indigenous knowers, and their experiential, cultural, situated knowledge. It might include a grasp of things a feminist science would see as having alternative evidence-based explanations.

Some Problems with Assessment

A different criticism of our current assessment tools comes from Aimée Knight's recent argument for an asset-based assessment approach to community development, that is, one focused on strengths rather than the community's deficits or on problems the institutional partner sets out to "solve." Like Adrienne Maree

---

attempt at control, but its basis in a "market discourse." In *Championing a Public Good: A Call to Advocate for Higher Education*, Commer explores a revealing repertoire of argument strategies that shaped this still unfinished argument (e.g., from dissociating quality from the market measures of quantity, to framing desired outcomes in terms of ethical values as opposed to technical expertise). At stake is the contest between a managerial frame for assessment versus the academic and humanistic values that support the public good in a deliberative democracy.

Brown, Knight prioritizes the slow work of building relationships versus critical mass. In her rich presentation of strategies and tools for building truly reciprocal relations, she argues that our current methods of evaluation put the university's gains (publications, grants, even student learning outcomes) over "community-building." (22). So in developing community partnerships she proposes three guiding principles: 1) focus on communities' strengths and assets, 2) prioritize co-creation of knowledge with partners, and 3) work towards change in the process of community work. (16) . And in her assessment of students, what matters is whether they are prepared to participate in civic life as "agents of social change" (49). She notes a pre/post survey that asked if the experience motivated them to subsequent community engagement and action, "more that 80% of students felt the experience 'greatly influenced their attitudes and beliefs about their capacity to create change'" (88). Did they do so?

In that spirit, the present study explores an alternative image of assessment based on cases that will let us test drive a variety of alternative assessment methods. First of all, such an image locates the meaning of the ideas one learns as John Dewey does: in the consequences of holding them, which will in turn demand a much more situated assessment of outcomes. Secondly, this Deweyan image of assessment captures a distinctive intellectual capacity that is best learned through communal activity. This is not to say that such capacities would not be "marketable," but Dewey's end-in-view is an education designed for citizenship. Such an education demands "a clear consciousness of a communal life" and activities "whose consequences are appreciated as . . . a good shared by all" (*The Public and its Problems* 149). The "training for citizenship," he observes, "is formal and nominal unless it develops the power of observation, analysis, and inference with respect to what makes up a social situation and the agencies through which it is modified" ("Ethical Principles" 127). Finally, by tracking the consequences of engagement at a more cognitive level, this image of assessment reveals some significant outcomes that are not limited to the direct *transfer* of knowledge, but as we will see, can entail students' *transformation* of that knowledge in response to emerging personal and community concerns.

Engaged education has a unique potential to fuse civic and social, personal and intellectual outcomes into an expansive version of the humanities. Discovering more ways to track these consequences of publicly engaged learning can, I believe, offer a new road map and tools in our search for public significance of the liberal arts in its "crisis." Helping build such a case is the focus of this study.

Making the Case for Engaged Education

For some, this engaged image, which extends what matters in the humanities, will seem perhaps too constraining compared to an unfettered life of the mind. In an impassioned defense of traditional scholarship, Kathleen McConnell's argument celebrates the freedom of academic professionals to do "academic inquiry

[that] serves rhetorical invention by acting as a placeholder for the unknown," which is expressed, as she defines it, as "endless gestures toward unspecified possibility" (52–53). This stance, she notes, is a clear departure "from more civic-minded, pragmatic notions [of invention] such as the one Hartelius seeks to revive . . . [through training] in rhetorical strategies" (52). E. Johanna Hartelius, to whom McConnell refers, does indeed define higher education's problem as precisely its lack of "relevance and responsiveness to societal exigencies" (153). Explicitly concerned with pedagogy, Hartelius argues that academic "silos" and the critical orientation that dominates education (focused on the "critical" analysis of texts and their ideology) won't prepare students to actually intervene as social agents. Hartelius' alternative builds on a rhetoric of classical invention and contemporary inquiry, situated in a "climate of exigency" (162). Here, in contrast to traditional acquisition, learning is shot through with uncertainty and ambiguity. In this situated and social space, students must build bridges between academic and lived knowledge. To deal with the problems this demand for inquiry and invention poses, her students are cast "as the agents of education" (171).

From a somewhat different perspective rooted in a feminist analysis of advocacy and leadership, Jane Detwiler, Margaret LaWare, and Patricia Wojahn argue that this elevation of scholarship (which privileges elite institutions) and the concomitant devaluation of teaching, much less "service," is a gendered choice. Their alternative vision of disciplinary leadership exhorts our field to create interdisciplinary collaborations with schools and community organizations. Even our graduate programs, some argue, "should be attending to the collaborative skills needed to build community-based research programs" (Miller and Murray 437).

The demand for an *engaged* education is raised a notch when we look at the situations students will face. Carolyn Commer's study of the Spellings controversy gives us an impressively actionable account of what "public-facing leadership" could look like when we choose to enter, as she says, "education policy-making, with the goal of helping those in higher education create new pathways for public engagement . . . [when we take] a *participant approach* to policy theory" (*Shaping Policy* 21). To do that, our students must be prepared to deal with the fact "that most education policy problems are fundamentally *rhetorical* problems. . . . because they are marked by uncertainty and require people to use language to appeal to particular audiences, to discover shared values, and to invite others to take particular actions that have material consequences" (*Championing* 4).

Garret Stack shows us how such mediation must work in environmental education, training students to become "transformative public advocates." To do this means working as "knowledge negotiators" facing a wide variety of arguments while at the same time drawing the public into "addressing conflict and re-framing a shared problem" (Stack and Flower 3).

In an extensive review of the "crisis discourse" in the liberal arts, Timothy Barouch and Brett Ommen pose the problem as a long-standing question of identity: Is rhetoric a critical discipline or a practical art? If the former, is its current version (which they say identifies scholarship with the discourse of a "negative critical stance") actually equipping students to negotiate "liberal public culture" (164)? Speaking from communication studies, they dissect the recent "genre of 'defenses of a liberal arts education'" that attempts to "*justify current educational practices* . . . rather than *consider changes to the tradition*" (162). They contrast rhetoric as a practical art with the "obstinacy" of continuing to identify our value with our critique of liberalism and contemporary culture—a stance which merely "presumes that knowledge of conditions of oppression will lead to emancipation" (168).

Barouch and Ommen's alternative to such education raises the bar from critique to actual engagement. Education for engagement would prepare us to face what Albert Hirschman calls the "successive eruption of problems and crises" that emerge in society and the "*steady diet of conflicts* that need to be addressed," which society must learn to "manage" (emphasis added, qtd. in Barouch and Ommen 170). Here, managing is the key.² Barouch and Ommen envision a "new mode of liberal art" built on developing rhetorical praxis, with the goal of "capacity-building as equipment for living within and among limits" (173). Their students, for instance, would demonstrate the ability not only to recognize the element of risk in any rhetorical act, but to respond with the socially required practice of "creation within constraints" (171).

Barouch and Ommen's expectation for a "concrete" response does point out a limit to the "inventional curriculum" Hartelius proposes, in which invention is the art of "creativity, discovery, and intellectual production" (173). Engaged rhetorical education can indeed offer "equipment for living" in the form of a rhetorical praxis that, attuned to conflict, builds the capacity to make wise choices in the face of uncertainty, risk, and limits (173). However, Barouch and Ommen also point out that this ideal of "equating invention with intellectual production" won't necessarily lead to change or "produce things in the broader world of contemporary liberal constraints"—unless we are also able to couple those "abstract ideas, general knowledge, and theory . . . [with] concrete objectives" (176). A good example of a "concrete" response would translate an idea or an ethic into a workable methodology. For example, Aja Y. Martinez argues that the use of "counterstories" from marginalized speakers hold "the potential for more democratic representation [that] honors diverse ways of knowing . . . and expanded civic participation to include historically silenced people" (28).

Celebrating the *Quarterly Journal of Speech*'s one hundredth year of publication, Robert Asen traces a similar "melioristic turn" in public sphere scholarship

---

2. Their language of "managing conflicts" may seem at odds with Janet Atwill's view of rhetoric as what she calls "a transgressive art," the art that transforms limits and conflicts into new pathways of possibility. However, what both these have in common is a situated art of responding to conflict with *praxis*, with reflection and action.

and its growing sense of mission. In moving from the traditional *application* of theory (which operates by "abstracting itself from the practices it seeks to understand"), this mission starts with a reflexive *critique* of its own methods and concepts. Moreover, it seeks to use theory not only to *read* the world but to *shape* it, which, it turns out, requires "recognizing the mutually informative relationship of theory and practice" (134). In line with this significant shift in speech and communication studies, Asen issues a methodological call for fieldwork and innovative methods that can, for instance, capture "the complexity and variety of relations between multiple publics" (141).

For Nathan Crick, engagements that shape the world involve the process of deliberation. Crick builds a rhetorical rationale for this next step, which takes us directly into the world of community engagement. With John Dewey, he would locate such rhetorical work in that liminal zone where the conflict between new situations and the comfort of habitus becomes illuminated by our impulse toward creative change. Setting this vision in tension with the status quo and its habits can "stimulate intelligent deliberation about possible lines of action in the future" (Crick 301). Rhetorical education can prepare students "by having them consciously encounter new situations . . . that stimulate the imagination and the will . . . [and] acts of intelligence" (302-3). In Crick's study, set in a rhetorical classroom, these conscious encounters can lead us into deliberation which, as Dewey envisions it, "concerns 'the nature of ordinary judgments upon what it is best or wise to do' or more precisely any 'dramatic rehearsal (in imagination) of various competing possible lines of action'" (qtd. in Crick 303). This educational ideal of deliberative rehearsal is further expanded to include Dewey's "ethic of communication—that is, an ethic that necessitates taking the perspective of others into account" (Crick 304). In Dewey, Martinez, Asen, and Crick, we see an expansive image of learning and that depends on encounters with others, with conflict, and the need to act.

Back in 2016, I was delighted to find that Crick's essay in *Rhetoric Society Quarterly* was placed next to an account of my own effort to put parts of this rhetorical pragmatist agenda into practice. Devoted to what I called "difference-driven inquiry," mine explored a series of community think tanks that organized and documented cross-cultural, cross-hierarchy problem-solving deliberations on a shared problem (Flower, "Difference-Driven," 318). Out of this growing "public turn" in writing studies, a rich body of research has offered new maps for documenting education for rhetorically based action.[3]

---

3. For a sense of the varied forms this move to engagement is taking, we might start with Thomas Miller and Joddy Murray's excellent introduction to a special issue of *College English*: "Reimaging Leadership after the Public Turn." Nancy Welch's unflinching analysis of the prospects for public rhetors in a resistant social climate sets a challenge: if, as her title asks, "the point is to change it," what are the links among service outreach, community engagement, and out and out activism? Steve Parks' fine account (and critique of the

Unseen Outcomes of Community Engaged Education

These lines of argument for engaged rhetorical education would integrate rhetoric's theoretical thinking and its pragmatic art with the challenges that mark contemporary culture and the risks, values, and uncertainty our students are facing. A pragmatic art would not consign the humanities to the limited (and limiting) paradigm of "course knowledge," which equates knowledge with what appears in texts, lectures, discussions, not to mention tests and papers, which can be easily evaluated. What one learns in rhetoric and composition would not, for instance, be exclusively identified with topics such as grammar, style, and genre, the history of rhetoric or its disciplinary concepts.

This is not to downplay the value and necessity of this sort of foundational knowledge at all. And acquiring this sort of knowledge is, of course, one outcome our institutional apparatus is already well designed to support and measure. On the other hand, the paradigm of engaged education takes students beyond recall, description, analysis, or critique by asking them to create *situated* knowledge through purposeful personal and public interaction with others. That is, it allows them to *integrate* their academic knowledge with experience in ways that will *instantiate, test, challenge, or adapt what they are learning.*

This book explores one particular version of this paradigm I will refer to as *community engaged education,* defined by its ability to create a dialogue between academic research and theory and experience, particularly experience with actual others who differ from oneself. Let me elaborate what these terms mean in this context. The theory, research, and academic arguments we investigate in a course can include powerful concepts, such as the rhetorical situation, transfer, contact zone, ideology, as well as theoretical perspectives, from feminism, cultural studies, or cognitive rhetoric. These are in turn linked to general methods, such as rhetorical, cultural, discourse, and/or activity analysis, and to the more specific tools of grounded-theory building, critical incident interviews, process tracing, or counterstories. When the academic theory one learns moves into engagement with a community (especially when that community is not one's own), experience becomes the educator. That is, engagement with others across difference initiates a dialogue that can teach the *situated* meaning(s) of a theory (such as *transfer*) by

---

limits) of my own form of community work argues for a switch to social activism with a laser-focus less on education than on a working-class network mobilizing specific, local, achievable political change ("Sinners Welcome"). Jeffrey Grabill and Ellen Cushman take inventive collaborative digital approaches to "being useful," while studies by John Ackerman and David Coogan, Nedra Reynolds and Johnathon Mauk take us into the nature of publics. For new research coming out of different engaged agendas, see Ashley Holmes on the practice of public pedagogy, Elenore Long on the challenging process of "early uptake" in building responsive community relations, Jennifer Clifton on rhetorically based community/classroom dialogues, and Rachel Shah (*Rewriting*) on reciprocal partnerships, and others we will see in our discussion of tools.

instantiating it in practice. At the same time, that dialogue may also challenge, reinterpret, or rewrite academic theory and its assumptions as well as generate new, more adequate understandings.

We see this paradigm of engaged education at work in multiple forms of public engagement from community literacy projects and writing centers to partnerships with schools, community centers, non-profits, tribal councils, and neighborhood activists. It speaks through multiple discourses, using writing, multimedia, web and digital tools, in academic and local publications, public forums, and community publishing. But beyond this evidence of an energetic civic "turn" in academic publications, its lasting educational value lies in its call to ground students' intellectual work in a practice of inquiry and deliberative dialogue beyond their home turf, and to do so in the service of wise action in the context of wider, diverse relationships. This kind of hybrid engagement, where research, theory and experiential learning take to the street together, cannot be limited to merely *participating* in service, local projects, or activism. Engaged education calls for a form of praxis built on an *intellectual/experiential dialogue*. And its larger end-in-view must be realized in *outcomes* which are not necessarily limited to material or political ones, but can include engaged public, civic, and community understandings built on that dialogue. Such understandings become ones a student can act on and take into their personal and professional life as well. Although our institutional apparatus is not well designed to track those outcomes beyond the classroom or make our case, new work on transfer can be one promising place to start.

How Does (Does?) an Education for Engagement Transfer?

Much of the contemporary discussion of educational outcomes is couched in the terms of transfer: Is prior knowledge carried over (or not) into new situations? Yet for all its clear importance, the nature of transfer is cloudy: Its meaning has undergone substantive re-conceptualizations and shifts in focus; its process and what triggers it are under debate; and the teaching or training designed to produce it has had mixed success. The research I have noted below reflects some of these critical points of disagreement. On the other hand, if we choose to read these differences as giving us what are inevitably *situated* accounts (rather than broadly inclusive *definitional* ones) we can uncover more useful evidence about the *varied* kinds of intellectual work, shaped by the particular tasks, contexts, and writing our students may face. And, I will argue, reading this research for its accounts of public consequences can also reveal some outcomes of *different* forms of engagement.

How Does Transfer Work?

Our traditional accounts of academic transfer (when it is not simply an automated thought triggered by association) involve applying skills you just learned whether it is to the next assignment or problem set, to a subsequent, more advanced class, to a related situation, or to an essentially new context in which perhaps only a few elements overlap. Perkins and Salomon say this process of transfer can motor down either a low road or a high road. Embarking on the high road typically calls for metacognition: actively attending to the cues that call up relevant knowledge. For example, suppose you have just been asked to conduct a cross-cultural interview and write up your interpretation of what transpired—a not uncommon task students will meet in all kinds of teamwork, counseling, consulting, or customer service. Of course, there *was* a discussion of this topic in your course readings, but in practice....

A central problem that troubles the transfer research is not the failure to dredge up or use prior classroom or school-based knowledge, but even noticing that it is relevant in a new situation. If the parallels are not explicit, it remains tacit (Bereiter "Knowledge"). In this cross-cultural encounter, our interviewer must not only notice the telling interactional cues (about cultural expectations, for instance) that might or might not call up past learning. She must then call on metacognition to apply it (which could also include an awareness of what she *doesn't* know or potentially problematic/inaccurate assumptions). When this takes the form of explicit declarative knowledge, metaknowledge might include what the interviewer has (or hasn't) learned about interview techniques, as well as connections to past experience, or to the challenge this particular intercultural situation may present. Meta*knowledge,* then, allows the interviewer to represent what they know in ways that lets them think, evaluate, or talk *about* it—if asked. The term meta*cognition,* on the other hand, refers to mental action. Although carried out at varying degrees of awareness, metacognition is the thinking act of calling up and knowingly applying a repertoire of skills and strategies, from a general skill of talking across difference, to strategies learned in a class, such as how to frame a problem or draw out the interviewee's situated knowledge. Metacognitive work can be the high-performance engine of transfer.

However, we should bear in mind that most studies of transfer in our area have been conducted on the transfer from first year writing to subsequent courses or from a course in professional writing to an internship. The unit of analysis is typically either a target task, or the writers themselves (often in terms of their "disposition" to transfer to not), or the contextual features that shape performance. These three foci (on the task, attitude, or context) may offer little insight into the rhetorical or strategic work of the writer. Compare this, for instance, to an approach to teaching transfer in which Craig Moreau starts by documenting the strategies for innovation used in actual workplace teams ("Teams"), translating those into teachable rhetorical moves and then tracking the (successful) transfer of these "practices for innovation rhetoric" in professional writing classes" ("Teaching" 12).

Moreover, recent research has argued that the notion of "transfer" itself is problematic, given its image of a static packet of knowledge to be applied relatively intact across tasks, as when the school genre of proposal-writing is neatly transferred to supposedly parallel tasks in an internship or job (nice work if you can get it). But in fact, these tasks are more likely to call, first, for the recognition that what you learned in school actually applies to the new situation (e.g., is *proposing* a new collaborative agenda to an inner-city community group likely to call up the proposal writing assignment you did in college?). In studies of transfer in technical areas, this recognition often meant discerning the "pragmatic relevance" of your "how-to" knowledge to new problems (Bassok and Holyoak 69). Second, even with an awareness of the connection, you will likely be forced to reconstruct what you do know for a typically new, context-bound purpose.

In an effort to go beyond the limits of transfer as direct importation of specific skills or genre features, researchers are proposing new metaphors and ways of conceptualizing transfer as a more constructive process.[4] The expanded act of transfer they document suggests a useful framework for tracking some of the outcomes of engaged education. It may demand the prior work of recontextualizing and integrating ideas across disciplines in which transfer is a rhetorical act (Nowacek). Or transfer might involve *repurposing knowledge* for a new task (Roozen). Or it may require *relearning how to write* and the various kinds of *transformation* Doug Brent's student interns had to undertake.[5] To cross that shadowy divide from school into a new multi-tasking, multi-reader rhetorical environment at work, they had to figure out how to translate their "academic skills into (workplace) practices" (589). To do so, Brent argued, required a repertoire of "highly general strategies for managing new tasks" (589) and "more principles and more conscious awareness of the rhetorical moves [they could] make" (590). Yet, as Brent points out, student writers were frequently unable to articulate these kinds of complex adaptive choices or strategies. The absence of articulation apparently makes a difference. When asked to revise a troubled publicity document, his inexperienced writers depended on the swift, automated slide into rewriting. The experienced writers, on the other hand, displayed the additional ability to recognize, often name, and reflect on choices and alternatives. Of course, the act of diagnosis is a cognitively expensive option. And in our process tracing studies of experts and novices revising, the experienced writers did not always turn to diagnosis. It was, however, what we soon dubbed as "the expert's option": a reflection of the writer's capacity for strategic choice when it was needed (Flower et al., "Detection" 47). And when writers must become, in Rebecca Nowacek's metaphor, "agents of integration," reshaping, repurposing, or resituating their knowledge, strategic choice becomes their ace in the hole.

---

4. The following studies offer helpful reviews of this literature, showing some of the different ways in which such transformations can be parsed: Elizabeth Wardle on repurposing ("Creative"); Doug Brent on transformative learning for internships; Anne Beaufort on mental schemas and heuristics (*College Writing*); Ryan Roderick on self-regulation; Kathleen Yancy on reflective meaning making (Introduction).

5. Useful parallels to this contrast in kinds of knowing appear in the work of developmental psychologists Scardamalia and Bereiter, who show how young writers must learn to move from what they call knowledge-telling to knowledge-transformation that takes a larger set of constraints into account (such as a reader's expectations).

In the atmosphere of challenge and uncertainty that often surrounds transfer, it is hardly surprising that a transformative effort will also involve a *disposition* or willingness to engage its demands (Roderick). Such a disposition is affected, as Neil Baird and Bradley Dilger show, not only by the student's expected return on the effort, but also by their sense of ownership and self-efficacy, as well as the easiness with which they face complexity or difficulty (706). Moreover, the past "knowledge" we call up is typically embedded in personal experience, often saturated with its associated affective elements, ranging from curiosity, *ah ha* moments, or confidence, to uncertainty, incompetence, or anxiety (Efklides). So to assess any act of transfer as a significant educational outcome, we must first consider the first consider the contextual, cognitive, and affective demands the individual had to deal with.

Challenging the Assumptions of "Transfer" Itself

At this point, our image of socially significant outcomes gets raised a notch as we begin to see how engaged classes that link academic theory with experience may support a kind of transfer that can reach across tasks, contexts, and time. King Beach enters this debate by significantly expanding the whole unit of analysis beyond the individual and/or the task, redefining transfer as a *sociocultural* interaction between people and their contexts (an interaction which can, in fact, change those relations). As in the case of cross-cultural interviews or a community/university collaboration, writers, whatever their prior knowledge, are being plunged into a network of dynamic, often contradictory forces. In such situations, transfer, as Beach reconceptualizes it, becomes a "consequential transition among social activities" (104). In practice, a transition means stepping beyond mere application of familiar practices into "the construction of new knowledge, identities, ways of knowing and new positionings of oneself in the world" (113). These transitions can become *consequential,* as he uses the term, "when they are consciously reflected on, often struggled with, and the eventual outcome changes one's sense of self and social positioning" (113–14). That is, when the consequence of this reconstruction is the alteration of actual interactions.

To get at another aspect of this complex dynamic, Elizabeth Wardle uses the concept of *creative repurposing*, in which students make the strategic choice to take a "problem-exploring" versus an "answer-getting" approach to new, ill-structured problems (1–2). In the problem-solving stance she observes, students question not only their own habits of mind, but assumptions derived from prior schooling. Like Beach, her theorizing is based on an expanded cognitive and socio-cultural image of learning developed in activity theory (a lens to which we will also turn).

For instance, these "consequential" situations (i.e., ones that demand creative or reconstructive thinking) often involve a shift from one setting or activity system to another, such as from school to work.[6] Or perhaps your situation is itself is in flux,

---

6. A recent fascinating review of transfer focused on teaching for "information

responding to new circumstances or to the impact of your own presence, strategies, ideas. (e.g., in the midst of conducting that cross-cultural interview, something appears to have triggered a new but hidden agenda for your interlocutor. Or halfway through a series of interviews on a community issue, you realize the focus of your own inquiry or perhaps the social/political climate for this cultural exchange has shifted.) You can no longer respond by merely "applying past knowledge" or genre cues but must actually figure out how best to engage in this shape-shifting, socially embedded literate practice on the spot, in the act of performing it.

Another force that generates a powerful stimulus to transfer—one that a community-engaged experience is uniquely designed to deliver—is an emotional investment in the writing. Exploring the experience of writers, Jonathan Alexander et al. draw a distinction between "affect" as merely a felt condition and "emotion" as "a type of feeling writers consciously ascribe to their composing process and writing lives" (566). Tracking what they call the "wayfinding" of post-college writers (that is, writers adapting and learning in the face of new, unexpected situations) they stress the impact emotion, disposition, and metacognition have on "long-term learning development and writing transfer" (569). One of the key impacts on transfer was "meaningful writing,"—experiencing "the potentiality of writing," the "opportunity to mobilize [it] for real-world interventions" and the emotional investment often linked to the process of inquiry and discovery (583).

What these studies highlight is not simply a difference in how one names the process of transfer, but the highly variable, distinctly situated acts these different researchers are tracking. So in the context of public engagement, it makes sense to look for the kind of high-road, highwire constructive work that might support a transformative transfer.

The irony of transfer research is that most of these studies, whatever aspect of the process they examine, tend to document that transfer fails as often as it succeeds (Wardle; Moore; Beaufort, "Reflection"). Even experienced writers have trouble with this portage, leading Chris Anson to argue that neither prior knowledge, a repertoire of general rhetorical strategies, nor meta-knowledge about the problem can replace evolving, experience-based learning. In fact, Ryan Roderick proposes that we should shift our attention away from the transfer of genre knowledge and its conventions and onto the student's adaptive capacity for "self-regulated learning," that is, "a writer's practices of recognizing, evaluating, and reacting to emerging accomplishments or problems" (414). In the face

---

literacy" shows us why community literacy earns a blue ribbon for transfer. Conducting their research across disciplines and contexts, this study first identifies four "themes that enhance learning": Preparation for Learning, Active Learning, Metacognition & Reflection, and Social Learning. Three of the four are hallmarks of community engaged education. In the following more detailed of review of sixteen areas of scholarship within each theme—eleven of the sixteen normally turn up in community-engaged projects (e.g., promote perspective taking; problem-based learning strategies, seeking out other's opinions) (Kuglitsch and Roberts, 22–23).

of new tasks, writers who reflect on their own performances can identify conflicts or difficulties, which may lead to significant changes in their goals, strategies, and motivations. They make it "consequential." In his comparative analysis of self-regulation, Roderick tracked writers' responses to problems or conflicts which triggered one of these moments of generative reflection. Although all these graduate students were writing center mentors who had received the same training, they handled their problems in strikingly different ways and with varying levels of adaptive success. Focusing on the successful mentors, he discovered the self-regulating strategies that made the difference entailed a reflective use of the problems themselves. These self-regulators spent thinking time framing the conflict, setting goals, and even envisioning a narrative of progress. In a second, fine-grained study of a student's transition from an MA to a PhD program in rhetoric, Roderick and Moreau saw how self-regulation not only helped the student develop genre knowledge, but construct a new scholarly identity (158).

Cognitive rhetoric offers insight into another transformative practice rooted in the fact that writers must construct (and frequently reconstruct) for themselves an understanding of what an assignment means or a situation demands. The internal "task representation" which experienced writers give themselves is not simply more rhetorically complex than those of novices, it is also likely to recognize conflicting readings of the situation and priorities they must deal with as well as appropriate practices. In effect, expert and novice writers often end up working on strikingly different self-constructed "assignments" (Flower, *Construction* 77). In technical domains, this adaptive, problem-framing expertise also shows up in the quality of one's knowledge representation, which includes seeing the rationales behind actions (Gott et al. 259). Knowing "how to" goes beyond possessing a standard procedure; it depends on a strategic representation of how things function, one which tells you when to use knowledge and why (267). Once again, the issue is not simply whether one uses prior knowledge, but when and how.

Research in psychology, seeking more expanded accounts of learning, can also help us articulate what an engaged education needs to deliver. The studies collected in Douglas Detterman and Robert Sternberg's aptly named *Transfer on Trial* acknowledge that the recall of course concepts/methods and the ability to apply them in a final paper or subsequent course is indeed a useful skill. However, the notion that what we transfer is a symbolic representation or packet of "knowledge" is thoroughly dismantled as an adequate indicator of learning. In an extensive review of educational research, James Greeno, Joyce Moore, and David Smith argue that because traditional approaches to transfer treat prior knowledge as a propositional or symbolic structure abstracted from context, these conceptualizations lack the explanatory power that activity-based theory and the data on situated cognition can offer. Moreover, this activity-based way of conceptualizing knowledge opens a new path for tracking the dynamics that create situated knowledge. Knowledge, they say, would be better understood as *"knowing"* rather than an invariant, stable property one possesses. Knowing "is relative to situations, an ability to interact with things and other people in various ways . . . In the view of situated cognition, we need to characterize knowing, reasoning, understanding and so on as relations between cognitive agents and situations . . . and learning is improvement in that ability" (99–100).

So what successful learners take away from their classes is not merely the theories, claims, or procedures we teach but models of agents and objects in interaction, knitted together with real-world knowledge, prior experience, and inferences. To transfer that dynamic *knowing* means recognizing the key parallels in a new situation, used as cues to construct an adapted, parallel model for how to interact in this new situation (Greeno et al. 145–55). From this perspective, it makes little sense to speak of the transfer of a knowledge *object* (such as a genre, theory, or practice) when the work in question is the *adaptation of knowing* acquired in school to a new situation in which success is gauged by interacting within a wider social and cognitive activity.

The argument here is that one distinctive outcome of a liberal arts education can be this style of "interactive knowing," which can support Beach's self-conscious, "consequential" transitions that reshape knowledge, relationships, and identity. It endows learners with Barouch and Ommen's *equipment for living*, such as Roderick's strategies for *self-regulation* in the face of problems (and how to represent them), or that hard-to-objectify *knowing* that guides interaction within a social, cognitive, and cultural activity system. An obvious inference from these accounts of transfer in action is that bringing classroom learning into the test bed of a shape-shifting, real world engagement, and reflecting on the feedback it can give is the high road to transfer. Community engagement offers the ideal place to develop this knowing. Nevertheless, to build a persuasive case for an engaged education, grounded in the interactive nature of learning, means that we will probably need new ways to recognize its presence in everyday life.[7]

An Expanded Image of Learning

Studies that work from an expanded image of learning itself frequently draw on activity theory—the legacy of Lev Vygotsky and the influential analytical paradigm of Yrjö Engeström that has stimulated research in psychology, sociology, management, education, and rhetoric. Locating learning and its uses within a more complex cognitive, social, cultural *activity system* lets us see how our disposition, generative problem-solving strategies, reflection, and metacognitive

---

7. For example, a typical study hoped to prove the impact of a new curriculum focused on global issues and empathy. Its measurement tool, a university-wide outcome assessment based on writing, showed no growth. However, researchers doing a thematic reading of these students' writing, were struck by another kind of knowing—the frequency of students' *reflection* "on their personal experiences" (Branson et. al. 302) Maybe, they suggest, "we had picked the wrong focus for the available . . . outcomes" (302).

awareness might interact with socially and culturally supplied tools, rules, and contexts. Doing so remaps the territory of outcomes, opening paths for assessing the dynamically interactive knowing engagement can create.

As we will see in the case studies and chapters that follow, activity analysis expands the unit of analysis in three dimensions. This lens directs our attention first to an agent acting on an object (e.g., a goal, task, or centering object and its attendant outcomes), which is in turn embedded in a community. Secondly, it calls us to locate these three elements (*agent, objects, and community*) within a larger activity system, which includes *rules, roles* (a division of labor including power and status), and *mediating tools* (both material and conceptual). Finally, and perhaps most importantly, this image of activity is characterized not only by the constant interaction among these elements but by *contradictions* or competing agendas between them. Attending to these contradictions turns out to be critical because they are most often the sites where innovation or change happens (Engeström "Developmental Studies"). In fact, as Engeström shows, it is when people attend to the challenges and contradictions within an activity system that they are most likely achieve what he calls "expansive learning," which *embraces* conflict. Unlike that image of transfer in which one inserts a packet of prior knowledge into the appropriate slot of a new task, in activity theory, prior knowledge is much more likely to walk into, as William James puts it, "the blooming, buzzing confusion" of an activity, where contradiction is not only likely, but a force that drives creative change (488).

This expanded unit of analysis grows out of Engeström's combined concern with social justice and highly situated research into the interactions of people at work. His influential framework for analyzing activity systems helps us see rhetorical action embedded, whether we realize it or not, in a network of social, cognitive, cultural, and material forces. It gives us a language for describing how those forces interact in organizations and intercultural or community contexts. And its call to uncover contradictions makes community voices and marginalized interpretations suddenly quite essential.

In response to the questions, insights, and arguments sketched above, this study hopes to reach beyond the limited world and measuring sticks of the classroom to add new pieces to the puzzle of education for engagement and the problem of articulating some of its outcomes. It starts with a reconceptualization of transfer—into an action located in the dynamic interaction between prior knowledge and new tasks, contexts, purposes, and people. This dynamic, in turn, supports a hypothesis about the distinctive potential of engaged education. By embedding the integration of academic and experiential knowledge within meaningful public action, we can uniquely prepare students for taking informed, critical personal agency *within* interpersonal collaboration in a world of complex, value-laden social interactions.

The framework of activity theory can also help extend this educational hypothesis by including a more elaborated, cognitive account of how writers both *interpret* the activity of learning (including its rules, roles, and tools) and *respond* with strategic choices. Secondly, in moving beyond the classroom to locate outcomes emerging from these more complex activities of collaborative and community engagement, our unit of analysis will shift from the tasks, genre knowledge, or other bodies of information associated with transfer to asking what kind of "knowing" *was constructed* by a given student and to what *effect*? That is, what does such education allow people to do in both thought and act? Finally, I will argue for conceptualizing our query at times in terms of not only transfer but in some impressive acts of *constructive transformation* as we will see students create new ideas and actions out of their learning.

The chapters which follow will build a case for the distinctive contribution a community-engaged education can make within this expanded image of learning and knowing. Doing so will call for new methods of tracking these broader, socially significant outcomes of learning. So, the case studies of each chapter will also explore a set of informal research methods for documenting what students are making out of an engaged course. Finally, my argument will include research that takes us beyond transfer to what we can describe as *transformations* by tracking what that combination of academic knowledge, experience, and collaborating across difference lets students create and do—sometimes years after the course. Drawing on these cases, we will conclude with an inquiry into what it could mean to teach for transformation.

Chapters 2 and 3 will explore a series of cases that show engaged students in action. These student participants built life tools and new understandings, raised questions, and altered institutional practices, supported by the metacognitive insight to name the change they saw. The cases will demonstrate ways of using the critical incident lens and interviews, comparative coding for frequency, as well as activity analysis, and data-based self-reflection.

Chapter 4 tracks students within an engaged class developing both metacognitive awareness of their own problematic interpretive frames and working theories for ways to change them. It will demonstrate tracking circulation and conflict, grounded-practical-theory building, frame analysis, pre/post comparisons using comparative statistics and visuals, methods of circulating students' results, and situated, re-interpretation by the students.

Chapter 5 will document outcomes in which students are transforming their learning into remarkably diverse personal and public actions. Using critical incident interviews carried out up to ten years after a course-based engaged experience, along with coding for leadership, and a comparison of their key insights with research, it will reveal a rich self-analysis of applied learning

Chapter 6 uses the frameworks of activity theory and grounded-theory building to explore two approaches to teaching not just for transfer but for transformation. It demonstrates how those frameworks can be used for analyzing one's rhetorical situation and collaboration, building a grounded theory, testing for metacognitive awareness, and teaching students to use those tools for themselves.

Chapter 2. Creating Personal Outcomes

If writing is indeed a public as well as a personal rhetorical act, one might wonder, what are the indicators of valued outcomes? The work on service-learning, however, shows how little attention we typically pay to public outcomes. In fact, as Paula Mathieu charges, institutional goals for constantly increasing student placement numbers lead universities to ignore (if not dismiss) community needs when they initiate and evaluate service-learning (Flower and Heath; Shah).

For some like Aaron Schutz and Ann Gere, these reports are an indictment of service-learning for its failure to raise students' cultural awareness and challenge their desire merely to help. And as Richard Bradley reminds us, "What gets measured gets done . . . If you can't see success, you can't reward it . . . If you can't recognize failure, you can't learn from it" (151). Not unlike the holistic claims and the search for a broad array of effects seen in the research on career education in the 1970s, on experiential education in the 1980s, and on service-learning in 1990s, the enduring finding seems to be that the specific things you teach, support, monitor, and measure are the ones students learn.

The ability to demonstrate public outcomes is especially important for programs tied to community development in which students can play a real role in public issues (Miller 107). And the non-profit community organizations with which we often work are regularly required to justify their funding from foundations in terms of outcomes. Yet as Teresa Redd's study of assessment in service learning showed, there can be "significant discrepancies in the teacher and client assessment stemming from different views of the rhetorical situation" (15). When we don't work to articulate the indicators we are working toward, teachers, partners and clients can disagree on what constitutes an effective public performance. So the next two chapters will use four case studies to explore four distinctive kinds of outcomes:

1. Building Everyday Life Tools
2. Constructing New Understandings and Open Questions
3. Altering Institutional Practice
4. Naming the Change You Want to See

Each case will move from a brief description of the activity system to a more detailed discussion of different conceptual and methodological tools educators can use to track outcomes, followed by a final discussion of what my collaborators and I in fact observed using these tools.

Case I: Building Everyday Life Tools

In a review of the research on service-learning, Robert Serow concludes, "The literature on program impact in particular seems to consist disproportionately of studies grounded in a single approach—namely, the statistical analysis of responses to surveys of short-term attitude change" (13). Moreover, the participants in these activities may hold contradictory goals. Faculty may be working toward goals of political empowerment framed as a "movement toward certain highly egalitarian political and economic objectives" (17). However, the students in Serow's extensive interviews appear more concerned with gaining personal empowerment and feelings of self-efficacy from helping (17). Serow sums up his broad overview of research and evaluation on service-learning by naming four desired outcomes. In addition to the traditional academic goals of "competence" and "understanding," students see service in terms of "participation" and "relationships," which they consider ends in themselves. And in qualitative and quantitative studies alike, the value of service-oriented community experience is typically measured by its ability to produce student reported gains in self-understanding, self-confidence, self-esteem, and, to a lesser extent, self-efficacy. These are desirable. However, little is said about the ability of service-learning to support democratic or deliberative action, transformed understanding, or social impact. In our first case, the exigence motivating assessment at Pittsburgh's Community Literacy Center was an upcoming foundation impact report and proposal for renewed funding.[1]

The Case

The Community Literacy Center as sketched in the Introduction was a community/university collaboration inviting teenagers in its urban neighborhood to write newsletters and hold public Community Conversations about issues that shaped their lives—issues ranging from risk and respect to pathways to work, school suspension policies, handling police encounters, or teen stress. It also brought Carnegie Mellon students into an intercultural relationship with the teenagers—not as tutors but as mentors to support teenagers writing from the expertise of their own experience.

However, in 1990, when we coined the term "community literacy" for our effort, philanthropic foundations equated the term "literacy" with the low-level, low-impact programs of adult literacy. And writing seemed less significant (read: less fundable) than typical projects related to teenage social behavior and school retention. So our five-year follow-up study had to justify this rhetorically based engagement, essentially reframing a standard assessment and its methods. And we wanted to do it in terms of outcomes for the teenagers themselves.

Using a Critical Incident Lens

This critical incident method of assessment was not the norm for service programs as Serow had described them. Although this case illustrates a rather simple

---

1. The Community Literacy Center and this report are described in more detail in Flower's *Community Literacy and the Rhetoric of Public Engagement*.

empirical method, what it attempts to capture is whether this educational, writing-based experience was still playing a role in the teenagers' lives a year after being in a six-week Community Literacy Center project. What, if anything, of their experience with literate empowerment would transfer to the markedly different activity systems of urban life and schools? The impact report, titled "Where Have We Come? What Have We Learned?", began by responding to the standard categories by which institutions measure effectiveness: school retention and grades, social behavior of youth (delinquency, pregnancy), jobs, and program participation (Flaxman and Orr).

For instance, it included figures on the unusually high level of school engagement by students who had participated with the CLC (88% attendance), supported by an assessment questionnaire in which seventy percent of what would be called "at-risk" students actually gave the *educational* activities at the CLC their highest ranking, a 5 on our scale of 1 to 5. These results were followed by empirical evidence of the program's public engagement and circulation, including its publications, contacts with local government and school administration, and especially one of the teen-led Community Conversations which (because the mayor attended) reached a TV news broadcast audience of nearly 4,000 Pittsburghers. Music to a funder's ears no doubt. But what about the teenagers themselves?

So our report tried to capture the teenagers' progress by tracking down 14 students who had participated in a CLC project a year prior to ask the question educational institutions rarely ask: Does this learning transfer to your life? To answer this question, we turned to structured critical incident interviews, designed to uncover more concrete accounts for something that really happened in place of an abstraction, generality, retrospective interpretation, or what the respondent thinks the researcher wants to hear (Flanagan). These interviews were conducted by Mrs. Baskins, the engaging African American co-director the students trusted, who initiated the interview by merely asking if they recalled any of the key problem-solving strategies we had taught through writing (e.g., strategies for analyzing problems, considering rival hypotheses (or *rivaling*), decision-making, collaboration, and community engagement). They then moved to the central open-ended critical incident interview question: *Can you describe any specific instances—actual events—in which you used what you learned at the CLC?*

The catch was, for their response to make it into the analysis, "yes" wasn't enough. The "critical incident" research method prompts people to bear down on a particular event or actual interaction with questions such as, "What happened next?" "What were you thinking?" "What did other people say?" We then counted as evidence only those comments that cited specific instances and examples describing how the teens had indeed *used* their CLC experience. The coded results indicated, somewhat to our surprise, that a year later, eighty percent of the teens (on average) were able to cite one or more codable instances of a specific literate strategy transferring to their lives, distributed across a variety of contexts, even their life plans.[2]

Table 2.1 Number of Teenagers Describing the Transfer of a Specific Literate Strategy

In School	At Home	In Society	On Life Plans	CLC's Transfer Index
13 = 93%	12 = 86%	11 = 79%	9 = 64%	80%

What We Observed

Excerpts from the recorded comments themselves, including those noted here, suggest the nature of this "transfer" and the extent to which the teens choose to use these literate practices, transforming them into ways to *respond differently* to the world around them—ranging from parents, teachers, and friends to the pressures of urban stress and even violence. For example, students Daryl and Jason talked about using the strategies to navigate difficult situations with family and at school:

> [On the Rivaling strategy]: "Before, when I had nowhere to go [for help], I couldn't say nothin' because nobody would listen. Before I wouldn't rival nobody; I thought it in my head, but couldn't talk."—Daryl

> [On the Story-Behind-the-Story strategy]: "When my brother & I didn't have a place to live and nobody would take us, I tried to understand their side—my aunt didn't have money; my dad had no room."—Daryl

> [On the Options and Outcomes Decision-Making strategy]: "After moving to a new neighborhood where white guys at school were overheard saying, "Niggers gonna come up here and take over," I could fight and get suspended, but I stop and think, if I don't, they might get caught and I go on. My friend always be fighting white kids. I tell him "just chill, be cool."—Jason

Although the impact report included the usual sorts of data collected on these teens, perhaps the most valuable aspect of tracking this sort of transformation is the way it shifts the locus of agency away from the program to the young people. It translates the conventional indicators of success (in which empowerment is

---

2. The bottom row of the table shows the number of students reporting a critical incident in which they used that strategy. Although we initially asked the participants briefly to recall any strategies they learned merely to prompt their memories, the coding was based on the conceptual cues rather than explicitly using any name we gave the strategy. The name of a strategy in italics was added for clarity, not mentioned at the time.

equated with behavioral norms) into acts of personal decision-making, reflective understanding, and rhetorical action. Compared to the metaphor of transferring (what *we* taught), the outcomes the teenagers report are better described as the kind of constructive cognitive acts we see in writers as they build new, "negotiated meanings" (Flower, *Construction*).

In sum, critical incident interviews can serve a number of purposes (Flanagan). First, as an assessment tool, they can focus on the students' own assessments of both the program's usefulness and the value of the distinctive experience the project offered (in this case, using writing to try out new problem-solving strategies). The interviews document a critical outcome: giving students new thinking tools and agency that they could actually put to use in choices that mattered. As a result, the report itself worked as an argument to funders advocating the lasting impacts of community-focused literacy. Finally, we discovered that as these teenagers were engaging in the interview itself, they appeared to be achieving a new level of metacognitive understanding of their own options. Tracking achievement can do more than justify our own practices. As a reflective, pedagogical moment, the interviews helped these students see and articulate their own agency as both learners and social actors—to an appreciative listener. In short, the interviews documented that these students were indeed building everyday life tools that mattered.

Case 2. Constructing New Understanding and Open Questions

Much of what we learned at the Community Literacy Center transferred to a variety of educational practices designed to shape academic engagement for college students as well as teenagers. One of these outcomes was a course in which an extended difference-driven public dialogue was used to translate theoretical concepts and rhetorical issues into actions.

The Case

The setting for this case study is the Leadership, Dialogue, and Change course in which a key theory studied by graduate and undergraduate students was Ronald Heifetz's model of "adaptive leadership" developed at Harvard's Kennedy School of Government. In this paradigm, leaders are defined not by a charismatic appeal that creates "followers" but by the ability to draw a community into facing its tough "adaptive" challenges: the ones that may call for learning, re-evaluation, and even a change in practice. Heifetz's work (which we studied in comparison with other models of social change, such as John Dewey and American Pragmatism, as well as the works of Martin Luther King, Jr., Cornel West, and Saul Alinsky) invited students to examine their own experience and their assumptions about what makes good leadership. Then they began to test theory against practice by organizing a Community Think Tank.

To gain insight into the students' personal takeaways, let me first sketch what the class was doing. To develop this particular Community Think Tank, the class took up the problems facing a little-recognized group on campus, first generation and/or working students as they navigated the culture and demands of a high-pressure, high price tag university. We choose to identify these people as "Independent students" to recognize both their situation and agency in the absence of support. In order to document these problems from multiple campus perspectives, the class conducted a series of "critical incident interviews" (Flanagan) to create a *Briefing Book* designed for participants based directly on the interviews and their research. (See Figure 2.1) They then used it to guide the subsequent set of roundtable problem-solving sessions with a cross-campus body of stakeholders. Drawing on some of the rhetorical strategies developed at the CLC, these Think Tanks used the *Briefing Book* as a prompt to help participants explore clearly different (sometimes outright conflicting) perspectives—giving special presence to the marginalized voices of Independent students in the Briefing *Book* and at the table. Over the course of several roundtables—in which administrators, counselors, and faculty worked face-to-face with a cross-section of students—the participants responded to and expanded competing representations of "the problem" as documented in the *Briefing Book*. As the group moved to proposing concrete Options for tackling these problems, they were asked to test their ideas by imagining possible alternative Outcomes. Having organized, moderated, and documented their Community Think Tank, the students then distributed and published their "Findings" on the Think Tank website.[3]

The outline in Figure 2.1 (from a related Think Tank) shows the structure of a *Briefing Book* sent to participants of a given Think Tank. Here my brief explanatory comments are added in [italics]. Its questions and quotations served as prompts for the discussion. It is included as a way to suggest the variety of literate acts this experience calls out.

The course gives us an example of socially engaged learning with a particularly strong emphasis on integrating theory, student research, and face-to-face collaboration across various kinds of differences. So, what was learned? In the present case, our insight into the sort of understanding individual students were developing is based on an end-of-the-semester, four-page written assignment discussing how they had applied what they had learned (i.e., taught themselves). These probing reflections reveal an adaptive, personally relevant constructive process in which it is easy to see how their learning was not limited to propositional knowledge or procedures, much less to simple transfer. In terms of David Greeno's et al. studies of situated cognition, these reflections turned out to describe an impact on students' "ability to interact with things and other people in a situation." The challenge is finding a way to display how Greeno's relational "knowing" (which will be different for every student) shows up in actual social experience (100).

---

3. For an overview of the Community Think Tank methods and published Findings, see www.cmu.edu/thinktank.

Briefing Book on The Culture of Stress at College: Public Talk, Personal Experience and Responses **Introduction: The Community Think Tank Process** This Think Tank is designed to create a cross-cultural cross-hierarchy dialogue....	
Part I. How People Talk about Stress The Problem Scenario: What's Going on Here? Professor X: Given this exam score, have you considered dropping... Josefina: That would make me part-time with no financial aid.... Professor:...	*An issue arising in the students' research is presented in as a brief scenario with examples of responses received in the interviews.*
The Story-Behand-the-Story What is Josefina thinking? Josefina: My parents will be so disappointed.... Other responses follow from a Professor, Parents, Student Life Advisor.	*Selected examples from the interviews serve as prompts for the group and ensure that some Independent students' versions get heard.*
What Is the Problem Here?	*Various interpretations from the interviews, included in the full Briefing Book as prompts for discussion included: Disappointing her family, a blow to identity, letting go of dreams, she is just an underprepared or first gen student, has no support network, exams don't reflect learning...*

Options and Outcomes:
Decision Point One: Confronting Disappointment
Option 1. It's Okay to Mess-Up
   Educational research says: Mis-stepping can open a dialogue...
   Friends will tell her...
   Outcomes: If she says this to the Professor, he might disagree and think...
Option 2. Experiment with Your Identity
   Students think: We feel so pressured to succeed from ourselves, profs....
   A Student thinks, "It would be cool if there were an anonymous forum...
   The Spanish Student Organization says: You would feel at home here...
   Outcomes: ???
	After the participants at the table add their differing perspectives on the problem (which will appear in the published Findings), they consider the Decision Points these have raised and turn to generating and testing some workable Options.

Figure 2.1. The structure of a Briefing Book.

Using Activity Analysis and Its Social, Cultural, and Cognitive Lens

Using Yrjö Engeström's influential model of an activity system offers a valuable roadmap for exploring socially embedded action. Focused on the critical forces at work within a particular social, cultural, historical, and cognitive system, activity analysis can reveal how these forces are interacting, shaping, and reshaping the activity itself. Researchers have studied activity systems within many contexts: for example, a classroom with genre expectations (Russell), a professional internship (Brent), a middle school trying to redesign its practice (Sannino), a traffic court (Engeström, "Tensions"), and a healthcare clinic wanting to improve coordination (Engeström, "Developmental").

Analysis works from the perspective of an agent or Subject within a given Community who is facing what activity theorists call an Object (i.e., a task, a set of goals, or a problem space), plus its Outcome(s). Having identified our Object, including our goals and their outcomes, an activity analysis asks us to examine the influence of three other critical forces within this particular system: its "Rules" (such as institutional traditions); its "Division of Labor" (which might be collaborative or dictated by hierarchy, status, or power); and finally, the less obvious force of what Lev Vygotsky called "Mediational Means" (Wertsch). Mediational means range from material tools (e.g., a pen vs. a typewriter vs. a computer for composition) to intellectual tools (e.g., concepts and practices). For this analysis, I refer to these three shaping forces as "Rules, Roles, and Tools."

In Figure 2.2, Engeström's elaborated model of an activity system works as a heuristic to identify some of the forces at work in a particular activity—in this case, his own action of preparing a speech for an international congress on activity theory (ISCRAT) ("Activity" 31). Here the straight lines merely indicate an interaction between parts of the system. However, the jagged lines indicate two "Contradictions" within the activity. The first exists between "the very challenging issues activity theory is facing *and* the rather weak instruments of collaboration and discussion at our disposal" (32). In the second, disciplinary silos (formed in the Division of Labor) come into a conflicted interaction with the group's attempt to collaborate on key issues or build new tools (sought in the outcome). It is important to note that when Contradictions arise in the activity *system*, the elements in conflict, like those of disciplinary cohorts, are likely to also be serving a useful purpose for *someone somewhere in the system.*

In fact, the real payoff in analyzing an activity system comes in uncovering both those Contradictions within the activity and how people deal with them. For instance, students may face a Contradiction in an encounter with faculty or university administrators, as when students' impulse to use a Tool (such as the energetic, generative practice of offering rivals and counter stories of personal experience during class) comes in conflict with certain social Rules (such as certain norms of deference or the attribution of expert knowledge to a professor in this hierarchical connection). A desire to avoid Contradictions may also explain why groups will turn a serious problem-posing deliberation into a mere "committee meeting" to avoid violating a Rule or convention of collegiality. For some students in the Leadership, Dialogue, and Change class, my request for a written reflection on ways they had put their experience to personal "use" contradicted their understanding of a graded "assignment" as a display of course knowledge, a course evaluation, or a summary of "what they liked" about the course. In contrast, from my point of view, assigning this reflective Tool was designed to help them articulate their learning as a path to metaknowledge and to give me insight as a teacher into the sort of knowledge they were constructing out of this experience.

When the Object of an activity is the creation of new knowledge, activity theory and American pragmatism locate the significance of that knowledge in its consequences. A written demonstration of what we have learned is, of course, a standard educational tool to both create and measure understanding. But in an engaged education, it is even more important to see new knowledge as itself a mediational tool which is evaluated not by its abstract rational structure or truth to nature but by its consequences for human activity. The value of knowledge is its transformational power (Engeström, "Innovative" 385). Moreover, as we will see in Chapter 3, the usefulness of Greeno's interactive knowing may not be obvious in advance (as when one is facing a final exam). But it may be mobilized (in the face of unanticipated exigency) as a mediational tool with a material effect. Can we demonstrate that powerful outcome?

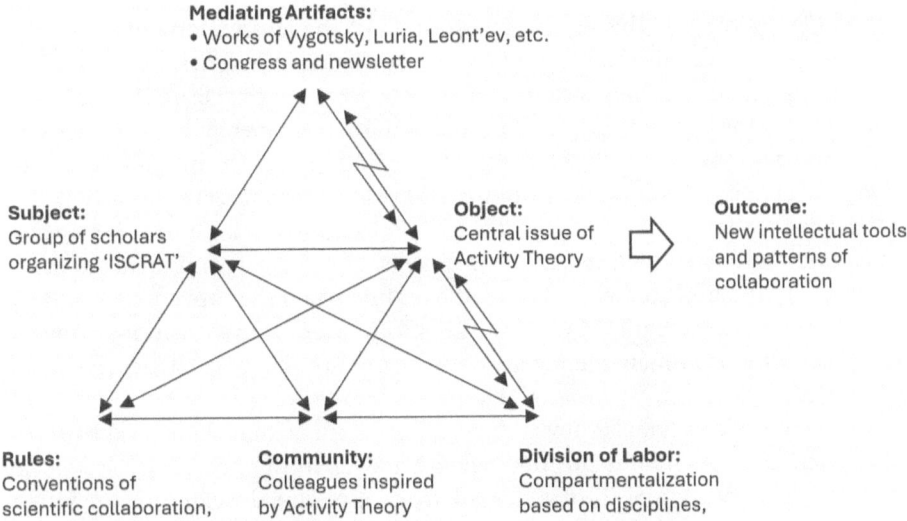

Figure 2.2. Engeström's elaborated model of an activity system. This figure is adapted from a figure that originally appeared in Activity Theory and Individual and Social Transformation: Perspectives on Activity Theory, *edited by Yrjö Engeström et al., Cambridge UP, 1999, p. 31. Reproduced with permission of The Licensor through PLSclear.*

Consider our desire to issue a call for change, given our country's intercultural context, with its deep-rooted cultural conflicts and history of social injustice. Although we may possess a new understanding, presenting that knowledge as a theory or critique that claims it is a new Truth is unlikely to be a change maker. Genuinely transformational knowledge causes a change in the way people, their Tools, and their worlds interact—a change in everyday practice itself.

A challenging set of criteria for building transformational knowledge in everyday settings is emerging from Engeström's studies of courtrooms, medical clinics, and work teams. The process he describes begins with "individual subjects questioning the accepted practice" ("Innovative" 383) and ends when an "initial simple idea is transformed into a complex object, a new form of practice" (382). People do not achieve consensus, he argues, through the force of a general argument, but when the germ of an idea *ascends*, in an ironic turn of phrase, "from the abstract to the concrete" and emerges as a coherent, workable action (382, 401). In a remarkable statement, he concludes that the outcome of knowledge building is the "creation of artifacts, production of novel social patterns, and expansive transformation of activity contexts" ("Activity" 27).

These transformations are "expansive" because they draw people with rival perspectives into communication that lets them reconceptualize the ways they are organized and interacting around a shared concern (Engeström, "Innovative" 373). Within this multi-vocal event, transformation produces "a re-orchestration of those voices, of the different viewpoints and approaches of the various participants" ("Activity" 35). The significant strength of the lens of activity analysis, I would argue, lies in this richly specified set of potential outcomes.

The implications of these criteria for change become even clearer when Engeström applies them, as we saw, to a familiar activity—the theory-building activity of researchers. The acid test of a theory according to activity analysis is its creative productivity—its "practical validity and relevance in interventions that aim at the construction of new models of activity" ("Activity" 35). But this is successful research with an added twist. Those novel social artifacts and forms of practice this activity produces are most significant first when they are created "jointly with the local participants" (35). And secondly, when those creations support the "possibility of human agency and transformation of social structures from below" (29).

The activity lens can also reveal how a Tool, such as the CLC's rival hypothesis stance, can also be transformed when it moves from one activity system to another. This conceptual Tool emerged from a National Science Foundation research project on "literacy in science" in which we asked how the notion of "rival hypothesis thinking" was understood and taught in different disciplines, from philosophy and rhetoric to social and hard sciences (Flower et al. *Learning to Rival*). The initial case studies conducted on this question revealed that while faculty in biology and history described how rival hypothesis thinking was central to their own theory and research, it was modeled only indirectly in their lectures, and their TAs never taught or mentioned it—though one said she used it as a benchmark to identify the "A" papers! So we designed a follow-up study with a group of (mostly under-prepared) entering college students to track the effect of directly teaching this interdisciplinary power tool. And it indeed produced some dramatic changes in the sophistication of arguments on a controversial topic and the ways in which they structured their writing (Flower et al. *Learning to Rival*).

At the university, this rival hypothesis move served primarily as a genre guide to critical essay writing. When we took it to the CLC, however, it was transformed into an important tool for collaborative planning, which let the mentors draw the teenage writers into rhetorical reflection by asking, "But what if someone else (e.g., your grandma, a gang member) said . . . ?" More significant was how the group itself transformed it into a tool for interpersonal interaction. If disagreement or argument is an honorable, standard MO in the academy, in the urban teenagers' world it was the basis for a fight or a sign of "dissing" your friends. And when our writers came to the table, disagreement effectively closed down serious discussion. That is, until the day the teenagers made rival hypothesis thinking their own tool by renaming it "rivaling" and using the announcement, "I'm just rivaling," to initiate energetic, no-threat group discussions. In effect, this transformed mediational tool allowed them to create a new, non-agonistic discourse for argument that allowed revealing conflicts to be drawn out and discussed.[4]

As this sketch suggests, an activity lens may reveal the way such influential and malleable mediational tools are being shaped by and in response to the system they inhabit. This was evident when other Community Think Tanks were convened around wider community problems (from the retention and training of low-wage nursing aids to the social price of revealing a learning disability in high school, to the culture of stress in college). Here the activity system's community, represented by the group at the roundtable, might include nursing home CEOs and supervisors as well as nursing aids, or, in another case, school counselors, teachers, and teens with a learning disability, or, in yet another, college administrators, faculty, and first-generation and working students. Facing the demanding task of intercultural and cross-hierarchy deliberation, the institutional dimensions and power relations shaping these activity systems (i.e., Rules and Roles) suddenly became more prominent, calling on our "Discourse" tools to mediate the situation in new ways. This capital D Discourse, as James Gee describes it, provides not simply a vocabulary but a set of "*saying (writing)-doing-being-valuing-believing combinations*" that identifies the speaker as a member of a group (526).

Differences in status and Discourse, then, tend to authorize not only who speaks but who is listened to. Here in our Community Think Tanks, rivaling was positioned as one of the imaginative "language games" everyone was asked to try—and

---

4. Interestingly, the research we used on decision making noted that the students rarely consider more than one option—however, it turns out that adults were not much better (Johnson 67).

the roundtable moderators could use it as a laughing challenge to participants. Like the Briefing Books, this mediational Tool gave voice and standing to marginalized participants by refusing to privilege the Discourse of policy, giving equal standing to narrative and the wisdom of experience. And when speakers were prompted to directly rival themselves, they frequently produced the most insightful counterarguments. For example, the human resource manager dealing with discrimination against a new welfare-to-work employee would propose her own standard, a professional HR move (e.g., just tell them to come to me). But when asked to rival that option, she knew exactly how it would play out—and fail—in the activity system she knew so well (where experienced employees would get to her first). Meanwhile, in a classroom, rivaling *oneself* became a spur to critical thinking and invention that created usable "working knowledge" (Flower, "Intercultural Knowledge Building).

Another example of a mediational tool which offers a lens on learning outcomes, is the reflective writing many teachers use to support learning and transfer (Yancey, "Introduction").[5] In Rebecca Nowacek's classroom study of transfer as "recontextualization," reflection in the from of lively discussions helped students to "integrate" their learning across different classes. Written reflection can reveal not only interactions and conflict within a learner's activity system but can reshape

---

5. It is important to note that the notion of reflection, which will come up in other cases, is a bit of a merry-go-round. Pick the color of your horse and it will take you up and down through the disciplines. In writing, one of the most useful reviews of reflection in varied contexts is Kathleen Blake Yancy's *A Rhetoric of Reflection.* Later when she expands reflective practice to assessment and digital portfolios in "It's Tagmemics and the Sex Pistols," she reminds us that "we have multiple definitions [of reflection]—ranging from metacognition, account of process, and self-assessment to synthesis, rhetorical explanation, and exploration" (268). For instance, the many guides to "critical reflection" in education ask writers to identify, question and assess their deeply held assumptions often with the intent to improve self-understanding or learning. But as it moves into community engagement, it also becomes a tool for cultural critique, to uncover social assumptions and practices that support oppression. Here an important distinction Gholdy Muhammad would make notes that *criticality* is more than just critical thinking. It is critical thinking about power, justice, equity, humanity, problem-solving, empowerment, marginalization and other criticality-related topics (84).

Some approaches to reflection outside our field have developed even more formal frameworks for analysis and training. In a relevant account of "experiential learning," which David Kolb describes as a "continuing inquiry into the nature of experience and the process of learning from it "(xviii), Kolb compares the Lewinian model of "action research and laboratory training" with a more familiar Deweyan "model of learning." In a relevant comparison, he notes how Lewin starts with observation while Dewey's process begins with purpose (32–33). A related methodology from sociology called "critical reflection," often draws on Jack Mezirow's theory of high-level transformative learning, which is widely used in adult education and human resource development. It is interesting to note, in Henriette Lungren and Rob Poell's detailed literature review of this model, they discovered "little agreement on how to operationalize reflection" (3).

those interactions as well. For example, the cognitive process of writing is often riddled with conflict (especially in better writers) as writers try to negotiate incompatible or competing expectations, conventions, personal goals and so on, while depending on habitual but sometimes poorly adapted strategies. The educational challenge is giving them a look at or insight into this drama. In a study with college students, we had used the tool of a data-based reflective analysis to let students track their own extended processes of creating a final paper. The data they collected from self-interviews, collaborative planning sessions, notes, and drafts revealed a crowd of internal and external voices giving them directions, which in turn emerged from their competing representations of the task, context, and often their own shifting goals. In response to these new insights, the students were able to articulate a virtual kaleidoscope of their own working theories and habitual but sometimes limited strategies for dealing with dilemmas (Flower, "What Does Cognitive"). One obvious outcome here for students was the development of a new sort of metaknowledge about themselves as writers and the ability to make more conscious choices. For me, the teacher, this lens offered new insight into students' "writing problems" and assumptions I could not have inferred. Using this form of written reflection has shaped both students' writing and my teaching (Flower, *Construction* 290).

In the following case, we will use two tools, the theoretical lens of activity systems and the mediational tool of data-based reflection to demonstrate a way to glimpse some of the outcomes of an engaged course as they are located in activity systems beyond the classroom.

What We Observed

Over the course of the last 20 years, the Carnegie Mellon Community Think Tanks developed an expanded set of discourse practices and mediational tools.[6] What the more recent Leadership, Dialogue, and Change course added to the set was a final four-page Personal Inquiry which asked students to "consolidate [your] best thinking on the rhetoric of leadership, dialogue, and change" and how it could be and was *actually being applied* to students' own experience.

---

   6. The projects and courses discussed throughout this book draw on a number of educational Tools—named practices that grew out of our research in cognitive rhetoric. These were then used and developed in CMU classes, at the Community Literacy Center and later in the Think Tanks. Ones mentioned here include Collaborative Planning (Flower, Construction, Flower, et. al. Making Thinking Visible) the Rival Hypothesis Stance or Rivaling (Flower, Long, Higgins), Problem Analysis, Stories-Behind-the-Story, Options and Outcomes (Flower, "Intercultural Knowledge," Community Literacy).

   In addition, some more theoretical notions (which were explicitly taught as expert actions, not just ideas) included Task Representation (Flower, et.al. Reading-to-Write), the Planner's Blackboard, Transforming Writer-Based Prose (Flower, Problem-Solving Strategies), Metacognitive Awareness of Problems, and Generative Conflict (Flower, Construction; "Difference-Driven Inquiry," "Hidden Frames") and Intercultural Inquiry (Flower, Community Literacy).

This final reflection, focused on application became an essential part of the course, assigned as an inquiry on the principle that students remember what they have taught-to and articulated-for themselves, especially in writing. The analysis in Table 2.1 operates on the assumption that students' ability to embed course content in their own activity systems is a strong indicator of learning and of how it is represented in their own experience. The analysis in Table 2.1 used the lens of activity theory (its Rules, Roles, and Tools) and the tool of reflection to build a bottom-up coding scheme designed to capture some ways students had translated the course experience into socially embedded thinking within activity systems outside class. The categories (created from reading these papers) name a set of sites students referred to when they wrote about how their learning has been applied. Their areas of application ranged from interpreting their own performance to understanding concepts, treating genres as actions, and shaping personal goals. As you can see, most students worked in only some of these areas, but overall, the nature of their representations document some distinctive outcomes of socially engaged learning.

Table 2.1. Sites where learning is applied and turned into action.

		Students	1	2	3	4	5	6	7	8	9	10	11
The Application of Theory or Learning Discussed in Reference to a Student's:	1	Own performance/ actions situated in a community, a course, a role, academic system		x	x	x	x	x	x	x	x	x	x
	2	Interactions with people, policies, (face to face, in role as leader)		x	x	x	x	x			x	x	x
	3	Conflict/dilemma from these interactions		x	x	x	x	x	x			x	x	x
	4	Course concepts (in actionable terms)		x	x	x	x	x	x	x		x	x
	5	Course Concepts (defined in narrative)		x	x		x	x		x		x	x
	6	Own experience		x	x	x	x	x	x			x	x	x
	7	New understanding of concept or action		x	x	x	x	x	x			x	
	8	Genre expectations/ writing practices		x	x		x	x					x
	9	Personal goals		x	x	?	x					x		
	10	Personal affect		x	x		x						x	x

You will note that Student 1 in Table 2.1 is the exception that may help prove the rule. An excellent student, her paper was a fine review of ideas attributed to sources but applied to abstract, undeveloped examples. Student 2, on the other hand—an experienced African American college activist working on her MA—starts her reflection with an anecdote from her own experience two months earlier with a local action group trying to reduce gun violence in Pittsburgh's inner city. However, she says, it was the Leadership, Dialogue, and Change course that "taught me how to *re-define* leadership as it relates to everyday people" and gave her insight into how they "could indeed make a tangible and provocative difference in their communities." Comments such as these, for example, would be coded as a #4 (defining concepts) and a #1 (own performance).

More revealing, though, is her account of learning "how to enter a multiplicative discourse with claims that have existed before me." The meaning of this assertion emerges in her account of an intellectual and experiential dilemma "in the move from reading and writing to action and writing . . . I felt a tension arise between my own ideological conceptions of problems and relating these abstractions to real, living audiences." She compares walking into the action group "thinking I was well-versed in community and police relations [which, in comparison to most college students, she was] and later beginning our Think Tank interviews with Independent (first-generation working) students." Here too, she entered the conversation "with my own assumptions on how interviewees would feel and which problems they would find most important. Being an 'independent' student myself, I assumed that I was in the know. I was wrong."

In this account, we see Student 2 translating her new understanding into local, rhetorical action and into a practice of leadership that confronts conflict even as it as it challenges her own habits and assumptions. Her text also suggests the intention to carry this new understanding forward after this class. Invoking Cornel West, David Coogan, and Ronald Heifetz, she describes using Think Tank practices as mediational tools: first, in her own activist work with Black teens, to uncover "situated knowledge" about cops with 14-year-old Tyvontae, and secondly, to "manage difficult people" at her own Think Tank roundtable. She describes the discovery of "useful methods for navigating . . . the transition from ideology to action . . . creating conversations with real audiences that bridge the gap between learning from literature and learning from the experiential knowledge of everyday people." An impressive outcome by any standard.

Perhaps it is not surprising to see this socially engaged student so consciously connecting her coursework to a social/cultural/cognitive activity system in which her learning is embedded. So it is useful to look at Student 3, whose equally self-conscious engagement with conflict takes the form of trying to design a guide for his teaching. As a first-year PhD student, Student 3 locates his personal inquiry, in fine academic manner, in "what I've observed to be a sort of 'generative dichotomy' in the literature on leadership" from Emerson and Freire to Alinsky and hooks. The question is, should a leader be raising consciousness or moving people to action? This intellectual dilemma is rather dramatically transformed, however, as he continues, "I struggled with trying to reconcile this dichotomy not only through reading our course materials, but especially as I was transitioning into a new leadership role as a first-year writing instructor this semester."

He narrates an open-ended story of trying—and failing—to help a student who had already failed the first-year course before. Taking our work on dealing with setbacks directly into their one-on-one meetings, he discovered that this "promising idea" of laying the issues out was increasingly perturbing. He noticed that "somehow, simply naming these problems seemed to make things more intimidating for this student." In retrospect (recalling the other class-derived practices of building a network of support and a plan for action), he envisions "one way that I could have potentially helped [the student] overcome this intimidation would be to suggest different types of strategies for action, rather than merely laying out what the current problems were." For him, learning is transformed into the aspirations for his own teaching career: "It's my ultimate hope that I can integrate this strategy into my own leadership praxis and teaching, as well—that I can strike the delicate balance of helping my students name the problems facing them without foreclosing the possibility of productive action and success."

Asking students to reflect on the uses to which they have put their learning can give us insight into how they actively transformed what they were "taught" in order to enter a new Community and adapt to a new situation, or demands and conflicts in the Roles, Rules, or Tools of its activity system. Perhaps more importantly, it draws the writer into what appears to be an ongoing, open-ended path of inquiry into meaningful consequences. These action-focused reflections become useful tools for enlarging the learning agendas students set for themselves in subsequent courses.

Using the lens of activity theory to examine these data-driven reflections let me articulate how my students were transforming learning into practice. And it shows how engagement beyond the readings and classroom was pushing them into adapting old, constructing new, and testing out mediational tools. And they are doing so in challenging situations that vary from eliciting insider information from a teenager to managing "difficult people" to mentoring a failing student. At the same time, they are themselves reflectively, expansively confronting issues of status and power while digging into contradictions in their own social practice and thinking. The next educational step beyond this outcome, which I would call *constructing new understanding and open questions*, is to discuss such results with the students and find ways to put the evidence of this learning outcome into wider circulation.

Adapting Methods

Both these methods work in a wide variety of contexts. As the subtitle of John Flanagan's 1954 article on "The Critical Incident Technique" puts it, it was "A

Technique for Investigating Problematic Activities from Multiple Perspectives." (It first proved its worth in 1941 by discovering why 1,000 pilot candidates were failing the flight test. Turns out it was the design of the instrument panel.) In a little more recent example of how it could be used, nursing training has some institutionally defined goals around "caring" and for turning experience into working knowledge. However, these hard to track professional skills are essential to assessing the effectiveness of the training. And STEM courses (typically focused on *professional* methods and those outcomes) frequently assign teamwork projects—but rarely teach teamwork as a professional skill. In this case, Craig Moreau turned to tracking teamwork strategies and their outcomes in some high performing professional workplaces (Teams). Focused on "teams that innovate," he not only discovered the powerful effect of "productive conflict" but built it into a classroom and online teaching guide, which he then tested in an experimental study—in which the power of productive conflict achieved statistical significance (Teaching). A fine example of integrating multiple methods.

Activity analysis would be an ideal tool for tracking students moving from a class or training program to a socially complex situation such as an internship, research project, or local organization. How much of that activity system, with its Rules, Roles, and Tools and how much of its Community and Goals are they as a Subject aware of and interacting with? Is there evidence of Engeström's "expansive transformation"? To reap the benefit of this analysis, you might also create a space for the class or group to use these categories to code their own written reflections, in order to discuss what they made of this analysis for themselves.

Chapter 3. Outcomes with a Public Face

The two cases in Chapter 2 revealed learning outcomes which may normally remain unseen. Some were surprising outcomes in which students transferred and even transformed what the combination of new ideas and experience had offered them to problematic personal, professional, and public lives. There, Case 1 suggested how a simple research tool, such as comparing easily coded critical incident interviews to what we hoped to teach, can give a clear measure of transfer to real-life situations. Case 2 drew on the rich, theoretically based tool of activity analysis to locate explicit instances of transfer in the social, cultural, cognitive context of an activity system. And in that case, when students worked out their own interpretations of outcome data, their collaborative work of tracking and discussing transformation became in itself a revealing educational experience—for everyone. Here, we turn to two cases in which engaged education can create a different set of public-facing outcomes. Despite their importance, they are also often more challenging to track.

Case 1: Altering Institutional Practice

This case returns to the Independent Student Think Tank (Chapter 2, Case 2) with a much harder challenge: how do you track a public impact, if there is any, that a course actually has? When the search for consequence shifts to the larger context of an institution or a community, we tend to ask, *what* is transferred: a report, an assessment, a tool, a program, and how? We can, of course, point to the literal publication of a text or the transfer of a "deliverable." On the other hand, tracking the less tangible outcomes, such as the possible impact of an altered discourse or the way a problem is framed, may require us to shift both our expectations and our methods. Like a tracker, we may need scatter vision to detect subtle movements in the trees, or the close, patient focus that eventually discerns the faint impression of a hoof. Many service projects do indeed see tangible, short-term effects and have developed a battery of useful tools to access attitudes and skills. However, the consequences of rhetorical engagement, of inquiry, and of deliberation are unlikely to be either direct or immediate. To begin with, such outcomes are neither defined nor produced according to our design specs but created according to the needs of our institutional or community partners. Unlike work teams or policymakers crafting coordinated action, the intentionally diverse set of folks who participate in community conversations, for instance, do so with the distinctive agendas dictated by their own activity system, and they go back home to its established set of goals, tasks, and practices. So the outcome—beyond the value of creating dialogue in the first place—is typically to be found in terms of each partner's own home agenda.

The Case

As the rhetorical exigence for the Community Literacy Center's Impact Report to funders suggested (Chapter 2, Case 1) showed, we may need to invent new, more-sensitive indicators of transformation and the categories of meaningful change that both students and collaborators can see. For example, in *Because We Live Here*, Eli Goldblatt's engaging, influential narrative of university/community program-building, he describes a year-long series of energetic coffeehouse conversations and plans with a community organizer from which the only apparent result was mutual insight and a strong relationship. No project emerged from those conversations, as urgent issues in the organizer's work took precedent. So why did their meaningful dialogue count as a significant outcome?

Likewise, Elenore Long's case studies open up the rarely studied, often-extended process she calls "early uptake"—the initial rhetorical art of listening and finding one's place in a community or local public (*A Responsive Rhetorical Art*). It's the work of figuring out, as Jeffrey Grabill puts it, "how to be useful" (Grabill 193). "Co-constructed among strangers . . . diverse stakeholders, value system, interests, practices and purpose," this responsive "attentive rhetoric . . . signals a shared stance within public dialogue that engaged the demands of contemporary public life" (Long, Responsive 15–16). But in this case, being useful stood in sharp contrast to the expected outcomes of a university outreach program. The community was a disorganized, physically, socially and linguistically divided body of refugees from the Sudanese diaspora who had been relocated to Phoenix. And the strategies its women employed to navigate these transnational social worlds were often criticized as maladaptive by the professionals, such as educational administrators who design academic "outreach" programs that reflect structural requirements for assimilation. And that was the outcome Long supposedly should have been achieving. However, her "early uptake" attention to women's lives suggested that it was not the women but the traditional institutional interventions that were out of synch with their reality (see Chapter 6 for what early uptake did achieve).

Stepping into such a vortex, the community educator is not only trying to find her own place but also trying to help create a place to work from—i.e., an inclusive, multilingual, deliberative network where people can find their voice, define their own agenda, and achieve small victories and incremental changes through collaborative inquiry and support. It takes the stance Long describes as a responsive rhetorical art—a techné of eliciting and interpreting a group's real concerns—to discover useful ways to enter. For educators like Long, milestones and outcomes on this nonlinear path can take unexpected shapes, such as learning how to artfully negotiate hurdles that the city's outreach programs themselves put in the way of actually useful learning—while at the same time facing somewhat similar cultural tensions within the South Sudanese diaspora. As Long documents, the ability to progressively influence these assumptions and support new frameworks for being useful may have longer-lasting consequences than the more-visible outcome of mounting a traditional "literacy" project. But how do you go public with extra-institutional outcomes like these? Do they count?

Another potential category of hard to see outcomes to consider are the reciprocal ones in which both partners are discovering/sharing something. The title of Eli Goldblatt and David Jolliffe's book, *Literacy as Conversation: Learning Networks in Urban and Rural Communities* names the underlying dynamic. Goldblatt quotes,

> James Britton's (1995, 140) brilliant phrase "shaping at the point of utterance" which as he says, "sets up a demand for further shaping." And for the kids coming to Philadelphia's non-profit community Tree House, it "affords a space for 'shaping' that involves composing and interpreting, speaking and listening in the company of others. Conversation, both written and oral . . . draws people together into mutually respectful relations". And in this case, "over the years, easily a hundred college students interacted with Tree House children and parents, plus hundreds of others the organization touches." (69)

Just as Long used her community participation to conceptualize the nature of a responsive art and design new forms of engagement, the projects Jennifer Clifton describes were designed to call a deliberative public of students and various community partners into being. She sketches a reciprocal alternative to the way argument is taught in English language arts and first year composition classrooms. Describing the contrast between a genre-driven practice of text production and the "public listening" that marks successful publics, she then sketches an alternative educational model of argument. The goal in this model is not to produce a formally supported "argument" but to orchestrate a literal "dialogue across difference." But this, which this was not what her department expected, created a controversy

The question, of course, is how do dialogues such as these lead to both personal and visible positive institutional change? On that path, two potent-yet-often-indirect outcomes of dialogue depend, first, on moving both partners into the stance of inquiry—that open-ended recognition that there are significant things we don't know and need to discover. And this, in turn, can lead to an internal "reframing" of our knowledge, which emerged in light of inquiry. Rhetoricians of all stripes strive to strategically "reframe" issues for an audience in the name of a public good or self-interest. Although in our case, the goal is to reframe by discovering what we didn't know in the first place. As we will see in Chapter 4, discussions across race and differences in the internal, situated knowledge each partner may possess can be an enormous, unrecognized, unarticulated barrier.

In this context, one of strongest arguments for a theoretically grounded methodology that is designed not just to create new "knowledge" but to also drive social change comes from Aja Y. Martinez in her chapter called, "A Case for Counterstory." As she explains it in the context of community engagement around race, this "critical race methodology includes a range of methods such as family history, biography, autoethnography, cuentos, testimonios, and counterstory (3). The technique, however, is secondary to its driving premise: this methodology "recognizes that experiential knowledge of people of color is legitimate and critical to understanding racism that is often well disguised in the rhetoric of normalized structural values and practices" (3). This disguise matters because:

> a majoritarian story distorts and silences the experiences of people of color and others distanced from the norms such stories reproduce. A standardized majoritarian methodology relies on stock stereotypes that covertly and overtly link people of color, women of color, and poverty with "bad," while emphasizing that white, middle- and/or upper-class people embody all that is "good." (23)

When the outcome of discovery is not merely information but the substantive reframing of a method of inquiry as she describes it, the impact can be both far-reaching and shared. In all of these studies, we see an array of non-material outcomes that emerge through talk, through social networks, and over time. Evaluating such outcomes will call for attunement to what John Dewey calls progressive "ends-in-view" rather than a fixed end or the point where activity ceases ("Nature of Aims"). And since institutional outcomes are rarely articulated as such, how can we recognize and argue for anything like a public, sociocultural "consequential transition" (Beach)?

Using the Lenses of Circulation, Conflict and Framing.

I admit to an academic attachment to measuring outcomes in terms of written documents, data, or organized public projects; these are satisfying and often influential. But a closer analysis of less obvious indicators—such as those Goldblatt, Long, Clifton, and Martinez describe—could reveal another level of meaningful learning for all of their participants. Studies of how rhetorically influenced change happens in publics and in organizations, for instance, would direct our attention to three areas in particular: expanding the reach of circulation, responding to sites of conflict, and, creating the new interpretive frames that build social networks.

One of the powerful ways rhetoric infiltrates a public and nudges change is through the circulation of ideas and identities. Circulation whether in print, media, tweets, or conversation—creates publics (not to be confused with the demographic models of publics created by marketers) (Hauser). A public, as Michael Warner so memorably argues in *Publics and Counter*publics, is created by mere attention which says, "Not only 'Let a public exist' but let it have this

Outcomes with a Public Face 51

character, speak this way, see the world this way . . . Run it up the flagpole and see who salutes" (114). One important outcome of educating for engagement would be whether such a public is created, and if so, what exactly has your action put into circulation? And why does it matter?

As we saw in Engeström's model of activity analysis (Chapter 2, Case 2), the potential for and the sites of change are often found in those jagged lines in Figure 2.2 that mark "contradictions" ("Developmental"). These are points of tension within a system or between alternative systems—whether the conflict is articulated and acknowledged or not. For example, the comfortable structures of habitus, such as standard institutional practices for informing students about loan regulations, normally do serve a purpose for someone. Yet they may be at odds with the support others who don't fit the norm, such as Independent students, actually need. And authority may be so fragmented across a university system that a more inclusive, coordinated plan is unlikely to emerge. However, it is these very points of contradiction in the system, Engeström argues, that offer openings and sites for change—when they are acknowledged. And as his research with healthcare providers and teachers shows, such recognition may only come after multiple flags are run up by persistent calls for attention (Engeström "Developmental"; "Teachers").

So what kinds of thinking can rhetoric put into circulation that will support the recognition of contradiction, conflict, and the need to change? First, unlike the more tangible innovations other disciplines can boast, these community-based deliberative events can be intentionally designed to draw out competing representations, assumptions, and values, as well as the conflicts they engender—to create a space for generative conflict. And in doing so, as in political or policy discourse, they often go beyond producing information to actually constructing and circulating new frames for thinking with. As policy analysts put it so well, by "socially constructing the problem situation, a frame 'provides conceptual coherence, a direction for action, a basis for persuasion, and a framework for the collection and analysis of data—order, action, rhetoric, and analysis'" (Rein and Schoen, qtd. in Fischer 144). As discursive constructions designed to do "meaning work," these new frames are unlike widely shared schemas or cultural "tool kits" already supplied by ideology, narratives, or myths. Rather, such frames are actively negotiated shared meanings that not only identify problems and possible solutions but motivate a response, creating a call to arms and a vocabulary of motive (Benford and Snow 613–618).

As these new guides to interpretation circulate through academic and community dialogue, they are also creating a local public, a newly constituted body of people paying attention, maybe even widening the scope of the public through talk, text, or citation. (Perhaps even this published discussion will extend the public drawn together around recognizing, investigating, and discussing the nature of some overlooked educational outcomes? Perhaps the frame of an "Independent" versus an "at-risk" or "under-prepared" student could reshape our image of the problem?) So an alternative way to follow the tracks of circulation is to map not only the "reading public" as Warner does but also the social networks being created: who is now talking to whom, and what is the topic of this potentially "reframed" conversation? In organizational studies, it has become a commonplace understanding that the coordination of work is typically negotiated in employee networks. Moreover, diversified personal networks improve performance and promote learning and innovation in the organization (Cross and Parker). Is it possible that community engagement gives academics a way to build new networks for us, our students, and partners.

Social media has an unprecedented power to create reading publics and social networks; however, as Phyllis Ryder points out, social media does not create "deliberative" publics. Described in Ryder's beautifully observed account of a nonprofit kitchen and support center for homeless folks, the savvy social networking of Miriam's Kitchen succeeds at what we expect—getting donations. However, Ryder shows how those exchanges achieve something more for their white, middle-class readers: their astute

> rhetorical work . . . brings fans, followers and their networks together as a public, one that adopts a particular attitude toward the conditions of homelessness, a particular understanding of their capacity to address those conditions, and a particular mode of interacting around those concerns. (Public 2.0 36)

When we look even further beyond a local site to the public writing emerging from community action, we can see not only multiple discourses but competing visions of democracy (Ryder *Rhetorics*).

Much of the research I've referred to calls on a variety of formal, sophisticated ways to conduct analyses of activity systems and their contradictions, patterns of circulation, frames, and intertextual references. In doing so, these formal studies both capture the ways ideas and practices morph and how they map the intricate links of social networks. My argument here, however, is that these concepts—such as activity systems, circulation, frames and intertextuality—can also offer more *informal* tools for tracking that can help all of us, students and faculty, better articulate the consequences of education for engagement and ways to support it.

Working in the spirit of *grounded-practical theory* as described by Robert Craig and Karen Tracy, such an inquiry would start with a perceived problem. On a disciplinary level, one such shared problem could be our failure to adequately articulate the impact of engagement in a rhetorically based education. At a more situated level—in this case, the Community Think Tank described in Chapter 2—the problem emerged as a contradiction within university practice. It seemed that the performance and experience of low-income, working, and/or first-generation (Independent) students was often misinterpreted as a failure on the students' part when perhaps it was simply not on the radar of those who could help. Unlike attempts to test a hypothesis or apply a pre-defined theoretical paradigm to interpret or critique a live situation, *grounded* practical-theory building starts with systematic listening, observing, and documenting.

In the case of students organizing this Community Think Tank, grounded-practical-theory building took the form of a difference-driven inquiry that collected critical incidents and alternative readings of what the "problem" really was, which could then be put in revealing dialogue with each other. Their own next step was a reconstruction or interpretation (a theory or normative ideal) of these situated accounts which met the constraint of being actually useful. This practical interpretive reconstruction, Craig and Tracy remind us, is not presuming to solve the problem but may, in fact, reveal uncertainty, unresolved tension, or even a counterfactual ideal—one which, as they found, might raise a "very basic question that has hardly been explored at all" (267).

What We Observed

The obvious sorts of milestones that mark the Think Tank's public life and its entry into a university's activity system emerged over a period of 22 years, just as the Community Literacy Center had evolved. Seen in retrospect, the CLC's model of community conversations progressively turned into more elaborately documented, deliberative, problem-solving projects published in reports and in training materials on the web and in new course curricula. Some of these resulting projects also became more clearly action oriented. Our *Decision Maker's Guide for Peer Mentoring*, for instance, was designed for students to talk through problems investigated in previous Think Tank *Findings*. You could say we "reconstituted" our grounded discoveries into a more "practical" or useful form, which we began to test with campus advisory groups.

Some indications of useful consequences were encouragingly direct, such as the letter our university president received from the president of a local African American union. It described the Think Tank experience as "tremendously beneficial to [his] personal growth and to the efficacy and prowess of [the union]." The union leader also credited the Think Tank with preparing union members to participate in an upcoming district analysis of its institution's troubled promotional process.

However, like many public deliberations, Think Tanks typically perform like a wheel in which every spoke (every participant) looks toward a shared deliberative center but is anchored to its home place on the rim—and that's where the real outcomes are located. Public recognition of a project is far less significant than the subsequent uses to which it is put by individuals. The knowledge, frames or practices we put into circulation did not simply transfer but had to be *transformed* into innovations or adaptations integrated into the practice of a counselor, a professor, or an administrator. And unlike crafted publicity, the path of circulation is often serendipitous, depending less on websites and publications than on email exchanges, meetings with administrators, and informal talk.

In the cases sketched here, perhaps the most critical things put into circulation were some *practical* frames for thinking with and acting upon. In contrast to the familiar "student life as usual" frame, one new frame that emerged from the Community Think Tank was an assertion that a "problem" not only exists on campus, but that *we*—faculty, staff, and students—are implicated in it. In Gary Fine and Brooke Harrington's study of "tiny publics," frames encourage participation in civic life by unpacking the meaning of events and making sense of what we are doing (344). In social movement scholarship, the process of constructing a collective action frame, heated by the competing schemas and expectations participants bring, is frequently a contested one. Yet the very interactive nature of that process can also result in a "negotiated shared meaning" (Benford and Snow 614). And in Long's "responsive rhetorical" process, the process can become a way to seek out "alternative ways of naming this potentially public issue" (189).

Frames such as that of the "struggling student" can do this work of ordering (or re-ordering) our experience into meaningful coherence because they supply assumptions, implications, and appropriate responses often embedded in scenarios (Fischer). That all-too-standard "struggling student" frame typically accounts for late papers, underdeveloped work, or failure to meet financial aid requirements in terms of academic ability/preparation, failure to take responsibility, or low motivation. It might prompt us to visualize these in the context of a "warning" meeting in our office. But the Think Tank's new frame signaled by the term "Independent students" called up new interpretations; ones that recognized the achievement of having to manage so many demands "on your own." It foregrounded the challenges of working 20 hours a week on top of classwork or the difficulty of navigating a complex financial aid system without a knowledgeable network of support at home or an accessible guide to the labyrinth on campus. Equally important, it relocated the problem from inside the student to a conflict within the system itself. Thinking with such a frame might move us to alter our next student conference to discuss that late paper's Story-Behind-the-Story, or ways to manage deadlines, or how to negotiate those team meetings that get scheduled during your work shift.

Engeström and his colleagues argue that when a group can bring itself to recognize contradictions within its own activity system, it can open the door to what they call "expansive transformations"—changes that embrace a larger, multi-faceted reality ("Introduction"). Their argument for describing learning as "expanding" is especially relevant to the workplace contexts they study and to community ones. To start with, "learning by expanding" is not limited to changes in individual cognition or even communication, even though it may often "lead to self-knowledge and truly widened consciousness" (4). However, "true expansion is always both internal and external, both mental and material" (7). Beginning with the recognition of conflict, expansive learning confronts alternatives and competing positions in order to *integrate conflict and contradiction in a new perspective*. Not limited to mere ideas, this expansive (ongoing) reconceptualization leads to new versions of collective activity and to tools that can, as Engeström says, push "cycle of the expansive transition forward... The practitioners have the task of facing and solving the contradictions of their activity system as they are identified and intensified along the voyage through the zone of proximal development" ("Activity" 22–23).

Now all that may seem a rather large order for a course or community project. Engeström's research on "learning-by-expanding" speaks to cases drawn not just from classrooms and workplaces but also from social movements and the history of science. Yet activity analysis can help us uncover indicators of this expansive style of learning that builds a connection to larger activities. So the question becomes: is our community-engaged education able to "transcend the context given" or generate a new material embodiment of our values ("Introduction" 4–5)?

We observed ways the roundtables, supported by the voices in Briefing Books, could provoke the representation of unrecognized conflicts. For example, two staff members at the Round Table blandly asserted the sufficiency of their office's standard financial aid practices (i.e., the information students needed was posted "somewhere" on their website). However, the Briefing Book already had a student's direct response to the inadequacy of this very practice. The discussion that followed and the subsequent published *Findings* were able to juxtapose this apparent contradiction as an invitation to further thought—and concrete change.

A related end-in-view could be whether a documented deliberative practice and its texts put not only ideas and expanded frames but a Discourse, in James Gee's sense, into circulation. Here, a Discourse works as one of those mediational tools that shifts the dynamics of an activity itself. In line with Long's argument for an unabashed rhetorical art, the Think Tank named, modeled, and offered how-to accounts of its tools. Sharing its practice with participants not only offered a rationale for this difference-driven inquiry but put a Discourse in circulation (Flower, "Difference-Driven Inquiry"). Its data-based, problem-focused Briefing Books, mediated roundtables, and rhetorical practices such as rivaling oneself and others promoted a friendly but focused, self-consciously experimental discourse. One participant, the head of a hospital division, remarked as he joined in a "rivaling" strategy session, "We need to try this at our board meetings." I don't know if he did. But circulation can be an unpredictable—if underground—current.

Frames and forms of discourse can show up in texts, but perhaps the most lasting impact in an institution is a network of concern—new relationships linked by new understandings, which may take unanticipated shapes. Ultimately the outcomes with the longest reach are the result of an expanding network of people drawn to a shared concern. For example, serendipity created an early institutional outcome when a dean in biological science, who valued her participation in an earlier set of roundtables in the spring, became the university's vice provost for education in the fall. In the coming year's administrative discussions, she was not only knowledgeable about issues the Think Tank had raised but had already begun thinking about how to address them. In effect, this connection also gave the Think Tank's work an informal letter of introduction to other university administrators.

The motivation for an unanticipated uptake by the Financial Aid office shows up in comments from an interview with the Director: "This all stems from the Think Tank . . . I was blown away by the dedication of the students at the Think Tank. I thought that their interest and commitment to the project was amazing. I left that day and said, 'We have to do something.'" They did. (And we, of course, then circulated those comments in a newsletter on campus progress, highlighting their new approach to offering financial aid.)

As should be clear, these outcomes are more subtle than the documentation that supports a successful marketing campaign. But from an activity point of view, the ability to put new frames or even a Discourse that speaks to systematic contradictions into circulation, accomplished over time, may be the norm, even if it is the less recognized road to expansive transformation. And of all the outcomes engaged educational courses can support, this is probably the hardest to track but may have the most extensive impact. The challenge is putting new frames, unarticulated contradictions, and evidence of this uptake itself into circulation.

Case 2: Naming the Change You Want to See

In this second case, we discovered how a standard academic outcome—a scored, pre/post evaluation of students' performance—turned into an opportunity for a transformative outcome. Six months after the on-campus Decision Makers mentoring project (sketched in the Introduction) had ended, its high school Scholars returned to discuss the scored "results" from the pre-test of their decision-making. In ways we hadn't anticipated, they turned that meeting into an opportunity to recognize and interpret a new aspect of their own growth and identity. In doing so, they proceeded not only to "rewrite" the meaning of those statistical results but used the articulated, situated knowledge they created to construct a new image of their own path forward.

The Case

Like many community projects, the Community Literacy Center (Chapter 2, Case 1) was not conceived to be institutionalized but to explore ways to make a visible difference through locally adapted, evolving, and transformable practices. Ten years later, the Decision Makers project took that philosophy and its associated practices to campus as part of a new course: Literacy: Educational Theory and Community Practice.[1] The course combined reading research and

---

1. Stacie Dojonovic of the Pittsburgh Public Schools had created the remarkable Start On Success program for these students. I was exceptionally fortunate to work with her and later Ashley McFall to engage these students.

studies in literacy with mentoring junior and senior high school students with a learning disability as they wrote about decision-making in their own lives. In the Decision Makers project, the earlier CLC practice of prompting teens to talk about complex problems moved into the university computer lab. Paired with our high school students one-on-one, the "Mentors" supported their Scholars (as the high school students were identified) in writing a personal Decision Maker's Journey Book. The booklet, which sported a self-designed personal-identity cover, was comprised of three chapters, all challenging the Scholars to describe and evaluate their own decisions. The first chapter asked them to describe a good decision, a bad decision, and an imagined alternative to the bad one. (That last part on alternatives was written after a revealing, often hilarious, session in which the other students—who didn't yet know how the story ended—tried to predict what the writer did do, good or bad, then brainstormed options he or she could have considered. It sent a powerful, often-needed message that a person did have alternatives). In the second chapter, the Scholars tried out different decision-making strategies (such as seeking rivals or imagining consequences) to analyze a difficult decision they were currently facing. Finally, in the last chapter, Scholars composed a self-addressed letter detailing where they wanted to be in their lives six months in the future.

To write their Journey Book, Mentors and Scholars used a computer program we designed called the Decision Makers Guide (Decision Makers). This on-line Guide served three purposes: first, in addition to the online Journey Book Guide, the program allowed us to collect and score a set of pre-and-post "Starting Point" and "Check Point Profiles," designed to gauge the sophistication of the Scholars' decision-making. Second, it offered a template in WORD for writing their Journey Book. In addition, by posing questions and offering generic prompts in the margins of each online chapter, it incited the high schoolers to think critically about their decisions and decision-making as they were writing—and in the process, learn a key set of decision-making strategies (e.g., naming the problem, giving reasons and rivals, facing roadblocks, and using focused reflection).[2] Finally, the computer program enabled the Scholars to print out their own Journey Books, replete with charts and tables visualizing the Scholars' growing decision-making skills over the course of the project.

High school students with different sorts of learning disabilities face both learning and social identity problems. As we discovered in a Community Think Tank on "Naming the LD Difference: Dilemmas in Dealing with Learning

---

2. A link to *Decision Makers* (found on the front page of the Think Tank website) gives users access to the seven steps in writing a *Journey Book*, writing prompts, and links to supportive pages for writing each chapter ("CMU Community Think Tank"). Unlike papers assigned as a course requirement this data from collaborating with public schools was covered with a University Child Protection Form, Letter to Parent or Guardian, and IRB clearance.

Disabilities" held with students, school administrators, teachers, and counselors, the disclosure of an LD is a double-edged sword. Getting institutional help brings with it the stigma of incompetence, causing students to go under cover with teachers and peers (Flower, "Going Public"). (Yet that Think Tank also revealed a dramatically new public stance a Scholar from a previous Decision Makers was now ready to take.) Beyond stigma, traditional forms of evaluation, with which the students are so familiar, are designed to certify what a student can't do and reinforce a standard of normalcy (Mehan). So in addition to helping these students articulate some of their own strengths in print, it was important for the Decision Makers project to show the Scholars' schools, parents, and employers real evidence of the Scholars' growth and competence in a critical adult capability—decision-making. Accordingly, I use this case to demonstrate how some traditional tools of statistical evaluation can produce evidence—but in this case for the purpose of showing what students can do.

Using Coding and Statistics

To track the changes in the Scholars' decision-making skills over the course of the project, we also asked each student to create a Starting Point Profile, done in the initial writing session, and a Check Point Profile, done roughly nine months later. Both Profiles—which asked the Scholars reflect on their internal and external strengths—started with a survey of the students' Network of Support (people to whom they could turn for help and advice), followed by a multiple-choice "Asset Assessment" of personal resources (ranging from connections with one's community to a history of dealing with peer pressure or thinking through hard choices).[3] More important for the evaluation of their decision making, the Profiles also asked Scholars to think about five areas of their experience (from education to personal relationships, using money and personal time to physical, emotional, and sexual health) and then briefly respond in writing to three questions related to each area: 1) what are your goals, problems, or values in this area; followed by 2) what are the changes you are working toward; and 3) finally, what steps are you taking to get there?

We designed these prompts to gauge their ability to articulate a decision at increasing levels of sophistication. And as the Check Point Profile was not a memory test, a short reminder of the decision-making strategies we had discussed during the project appeared in the sidebar (see Appendix 3,1 for details). Our coding—tested for reliability—of replies to the three questions was straightforward. It gave its top score to a "Reasoned, Reflective Decision." This was an account of their decision that included "Reasons," "Specifics" (rather than generalizations), "Rivals" (alternatives or reasons against), "Consequences," and/or "Conditions" (including

---

3. The asset questions were drawn from the research of the Search Institute (searchinstitute.org) on the assets associated with healthy personal development and behaviors.

possible "Roadblocks") and "Qualifications"). A good but more limited decision at the next level was coded as "Supports Action/Developed," followed by a "Commonsense/General" account, down to a "None/No Fit" option (see Appendix 3.2).

Focused, informal research like this allows the researcher to show progress, make comparisons, and raise good questions. Unlike a more general qualitative analysis or a grade, it can identify specific, if challenging, actions or rhetorical moves an educator is working toward and share them with the students. In the context of this case study, it required a meaningful pre-and-post writing task and an explicit coding scheme that could identify the presence or absence of the decision-making moves we were teaching. The computer program made scoring the moves (and checking for them with another coder) easy. The coding rubric (on which co-coders achieved a significant 80% reliability) let us translate the score into four levels of sophistication in Reflective Decision Making, noted above. Then, the results were turned into a readable bar graph comparing possible and actual scores, as well as a pie chart showing the percent of comments each student was making at each level (see Appendix 3l2). This report was then available to each Scholar.

Making Sense of the Results

This use of straightforward statistical data differs in important ways from formal educational research. Unlike a well-designed experiment using the results to test the effectiveness of a specific teaching method, for instance, there is no control group and far too many variables in this small sample to make a statistically significant claim for either our methods or community engagement. (Maybe the gains in decision-making ability we saw in the students' Check Point Profiles were just the effects of maturation?) But informal research like this provides the kind of evidence that, given a clear focus and a coding rubric tested for reliability, can support a strong, reasoned argument. In this case, it is an argument for socially engaged learning and its ability to combine its focus on a critical adult skill such as decision-making with a small (but mighty) set of moves (e.g., giving reasons and specific details, rivaling, considering roadblocks, conditions and qualifications). These moves, drawn from research on writing, argumentation, and decision-making, were then named, discussed, and applied to decisions meaningful to the writer in a mentored, social experience. If we can combine this explicit focus with a significant change in the teenagers' ability to articulate their own thinking about a decision, we have a strong argument for a genuinely useful outcome—based here on the lens of documentation. In the present case, this visible, statistical evidence let us make a strong public statement about the thoughtful problem-solving capabilities of these students. And, unlike an experimental study, it made little difference whether we proved that our program was the sole cause or not. Especially for these students it was the demonstrated outcome that mattered.

However, at this point an additional "engaged" analysis let us go beyond a standard statistical lens to an interpretive one, based on an interactive inquiry with the Scholars (which also triangulated our interpretations). This collaborative analysis began when we invited that year's cohort of Scholars to return campus to discuss their personal scores and compare their school's score to other schools. The goal of the meeting was to explore *why* the personal and group scores differed, from their insider perspective. The questions on the table were "How do *you* interpret your results?", "What did you mean when you wrote that?", "Why is it these various differences exist (where you scored high on one area or low in another, or between you and other students, or between schools)?", "What do you think your decision-making looks like now, six months later?", and "What would you like to change?" Bringing this additional interpretive lens to the data had some unexpected outcomes.

A collaborative, interpretive lens complements and complicates the initial results by refusing to take the numbers, scores, and statistical patterns at face value as comprehensive indicators of growth. Instead, it uses that data as the ground for inquiry into a fuller understanding. The results of the scoring posed an interpretive problem to be solved: what did a student's written responses actually mean? What was behind that? Where is the opening for change or growth? Approaching the data through a collaborative group analysis asked the Scholars themselves to take on the job of interpreting what the Profile questions meant in their context. What choices did their scores reflect? How would (would?) seeing other options affect their plans for action and change?

Each of these ways of using statistics to look at outcomes has its own strength. But used together, they show us how engaged learning can build a public case for its outcomes and at the same time push all its partners to articulate new insights. The challenge is designing an assessment that retains the persuasive, visual, and circulatory power of statistics but without the goal of ranking the intellectual or personal worth of some above others. Rather, it is a tool for an experientially grounded reflection that affirms students' dignity and potential.

What We Observed

The Power of Documentation and Numbers

This form of tracking had two distinctive outcomes. The most obvious was the ability to create a visually persuasive documentation of growth in a highly valued adult ability: to make reasoned and reflective decisions in the face of significant choices. The use of focused documentation and coding let us create four representations of student performance:

1. The number of people in a student's Support Network—for whom they could offer a reason why that person mattered.
2. A bar graph showing each Scholar's self-rated level of social, experiential Assets (e.g., a history of dealing with difference or motivation in school). An

additional bar graph grouped the 22 Asset questions into four major categories (relations with adults; agency and responsibility; attitudes and motivation, planning and decision-making, and dealing with others), letting each Scholar and each school compare their level of Assets with their cohort.[4]
3. Most revealing, a pie chart showing what percent of the student's pre- and post-statements fell into each of the four levels of reflective decision-making.
4. And finally, a simple bar graph that let Scholars compare their own score to what they could achieve if all their comments were a Reasoned Reflective choice.

We then compiled the results into a second small booklet for each Scholar and a more general one for each school with an explanation of the project which we distributed via print, PDF, and website in order to reach out to parents, teachers, and counselors. The booklet even appeared at some of the schools' annual exhibit events. Both the analysis and documents were cheap to make and easy to circulate (Appendix 3.2). The significance of circulation coupled with these somewhat formal results was clearly evident in the case of a Scholar, Jonathan. A high-performing student on the autism spectrum, he had been supported (and smothered, it seemed) by wealthy parents. Coming to campus on his own (without his aide) was a new experience in independence that gave him an enlarged sense of agency. Jonathan's parents were not going to allow him to move away for college (even though his preferred college could accommodate his disabilities). But as his school counselor told us, Jonathan's newfound sense of himself, combined with the formal evidence from the Decision Makers project, persuaded his parents to change their minds. Thus, this talented young person could now pursue his chosen path toward college and independence.

The Power of Interpretation

Another important, but less visible, rewarding outcome for the Scholars was the practice of interpreting the scoring—themselves. Coming back to campus to review their Profile results, we initially began by working as a group to score and discuss a sample of high- and low-scoring results from a previous project. But as we probed the differences, the teenagers began to explore and compare possible options, see new possibilities, and draw out the reasoning behind both good and bad choices. They then used this experience to interpret their own comments and scores. This collaborative analysis created a fascinating platform for interpretive action where Scholars could articulate their own goals and strategies as part of a socially shared inquiry. (I would add, their unexpected explanations and reasoning also influenced the interpretive frames of all of us, including the teachers, at the table.)

---

4. The set of Search Institute Assets we selected for this evaluation were ones a student could choose to acquire.

This set of interpretive outcomes was discovered rather than planned for. Although we had prepared some questions based on the initial scores, what mattered was how the students read these responses rather than how the institution scored them. After that, these roundtable talks held after each project became an educational invitation to interpretation, inquiry, and planning. For example, the eighth Asset Assessment question in the Starting Point Profile had asked students to rate themselves on a scale of 1–5 on this statement: "In conversations with adults, I can communicate my goals and my strengths in ways that they can understand." In one not atypical case, both schools in this cohort gave themselves low scores on this Asset question: 2.2 and 2.4 out of 5. It sparked an animated analysis of what those numbers really meant, starting with our question: "What does it mean to communicate goals and strengths with authority? Exactly how do you do that?" Everyone was seeing and naming new possibilities. Eventually, those questions lead to others: "So why are both groups low on communication strategies?" But for the teachers, perhaps the most instructive result was insight these upperclassmen had into the question: "What strategies do younger tenth graders actually use?" I would say, the outcome that may matter most here is not the particular answers, though often surprising, but the shared, self-conscious reflective thought this opportunity stimulated.

The scoring of Asset Question 19 raised an issue which often comes up for students with learning disabilities. "When I enter unfamiliar situations (where people have new expectations of me or confusing ways of explaining things), I am good at finding out all the things I need to know." It had received a low score of 2.7 and 2.2 from two high schools. We asked the teens: "Why is that? So how could you make that a strength? Anybody got good strategies?" Our request to interpret this data shifted authority to where the real interpretive expertise lay: with the students. It turned the limits of a written and scored assessment into a powerful tool for metacognitive work and shared learning.

So the really fruitful discussion began when the Scholars began interpretating and scoring responses to the written section of the Profile and its questions, such as, "What I am working on in my life?" and, "What are my goals and plans for achieving them?" Many Starting Point Profiles had relied on Level 1 *common sense* statements such as:

> I would like to make friends in my neighborhood.
>
> I want to go to college.

But, we asked the group, how would you evaluate the following statement (drawn from previous Profiles)?

> I want to do better in school, **because I know that if I keep getting bad grades, I won't be able to get into college. You have to work hard to get ahead in life.**

As the discussion drew out, key terms (here in bold) became cues as to why this statement works at a Level 2: it provides reasons and specifics, such as examples or steps, that make it a plan that could support action. Students saw the relevance to plans like the one below, which dealt with the everyday realities of a crowded household.

> I am going to **study every day after school at my desk in my room, with the radio turned off and my brothers and sisters not allowed to come in and bother me.**

Discussing the final example below served an additional purpose of letting students articulate just what it was that made this example into a more-fully packed Level 3. As we saw for the college students in Chapter 2, Case 2, being able to name and explain your intuitions and insights can make them both operational and open to reflection.

> I could get a job doing fast food. On the other hand, [Rivals] that kind of job doesn't pay much money. Doing something, even volunteering, with computers might not pay a lot either, [Consequences] but it might lead me to a job that makes a lot of money and would look good on my resume [Reasons].

Using the additional criteria that can support Reflective Action, the group then began to imagine possible Conditions, noticing how the words "if . . . then" could open up an inquiry into what those Conditions might be. The criteria of Reflection also turned up questions such as, "Is there a pattern in how I choose jobs?" Interpreting these scores went beyond text-based analysis, as it let students talk about why they made the choices they made, and led them to articulate the conditions and qualifications that affect their choices.

> I have to start asking my teachers for help at school when I'm having a problem. Before, I thought that asking my teachers would make me look stupid because my dad always hates it when I ask him questions. But now I know teachers are really there to help me.

This statement reveals the student's knowledge that even good decisions will meet roadblocks. The next statement shows a similar awareness, plus the willingness to take an experimental stance to a problem.

> One change I would like to make is to be more giving to my parents. But my parents aren't always good to me and maybe that's why I'm not always nice to them, but I'm still going to be nice to them and if I do that maybe they'll learn from my example.

The responses also brought issues in the social environments of schools up for discussion, leading to questions such as, why did this school score differently from mine?

To sum up, a fairly simple statistical analysis let us showcase the achievement of these students in a meaningful, accessible, and visually inviting way to a diverse community. At the same time, it created an opportunity to critically interpret an assessment and its scores in a way that privileged their insider knowledge, created new insights, offered exposure to rival readings and the recognition of a personal application. In the open-endedness of this interpretive analysis, the students were teaching themselves those reflective moves—what they could mean, how to recognize them, and the words that helped you try one out.

Later in the project, another outcome emerged. We had been noticing something unusual about the Scholars' personally focused writing on campus and its contrast to that at the neighborhood-based CLC, with its issue-centered work done in an inner-city social atmosphere on the writers' home turf. We were somewhat surprised to find how quickly the Decision Maker Scholars on campus were disposed to disclose (and write about) serious, personal dilemmas, from issues of gender identity to *projected* "unavoidable" fights with family members, peers, and teachers. (Sometimes these dilemmas precipitated small group discussions around the computer, which actually reinterpreted the "unavoidable" into better options.) We suspect that the Scholars' openness to raising and writing about such sensitive topics with their Mentors stemmed in part from Decision Makers' on-campus, computer-supported, one-on-one design, as well as its specific focus on personal decisions. By contrast, the atmosphere at the CLC and its focus on public issues tended to be much more teen-dominated and community-based. Perhaps the privacy of on-campus writing, combined with the Decision Makers' increased focus on quiet personal agency, primed the Scholars to put their deepest, most pressing dilemmas forward for analysis. At the same time, it was probably at the expense of an invigorated sense of a public voice and agency.

Finally, in my judgment, the consistently most-significant outcome of the entire Decision Makers project has been the transformation of students' perceptions of themselves as indeed decision makers in their own lives, often in ways they hadn't acknowledged before. Whether a decision was for good or for ill, a recognition of your agency brings with it a sense of responsibility—and often a change in the perception others have of you. By tracking participants' performance in statistical, graphic ways, we can give persuasive visibility to internal strengths and growth. And at the same time, the scoring may play an even more important role when it is interpreted by the writers themselves in a social context that supports articulation in the midst of rivals, reasons, and options from your peers. This less visible outcome is likely to be a new level of metacognitive awareness and knowing.

Appendix 3.1. Sketch of the Starting and Check Point Profiles

This overview of the Profiles shows its structure and key questions.

The Starting Point Profile

This computer questionnaire asked students to create four Snapshots of themselves, typing each reply in small, expanding boxes to encourage a focused response.

Snapshot 1. Who is Traveling with Me? (Network of Support)

The Profile asked for a brief written response: "Who are the key people you see as a part of your personal network and a reason they matter?"

Snapshot 2. What Am I Working on in My Life Right Now?

1. In learning and education
2. In personal & community relationships
3. In making, budgeting, and using money
4. In personal time and recreation
5. In physical, emotional, and sexual health

Under each of these five topics there were three expandable boxes asking for a short, written response addressing: "What matters to me in this area? What values or goals or problems am I working on in my life?" And then: "What specific steps am I taking to reach my goals or act on what I care about?" How they articulated their answers showed both their goals and concerns and the level of awareness and control visible in their response. These written responses would be the basis for coding their level of reflective decision making.

Snapshot 3. What is My Situation?

Based on research into markers for healthy personal development in adolescents by the Search Institute (https://searchinstitute.org/), this Snapshot asked students to rate the level of their "personal assets" from 1 to 4, in response to 22 options such as, "I am connected to a church or club where a young person can play a useful role in their community," or "I have a history of handling negative peer pressure, especially in difficult situations."

Snapshot 4. A Letter to Myself

Finally, the Starting Point Profile is rounded out with some forward-thinking questions, asking the writer to name a change they would like to make in three areas: 1) my network of support; 2) my goals or values; and 3) in building two personal assets." The challenge comes when they are asked to make their decision-making operational by using the two response boxes to describe: "1) Some steps I think I can take to make that change are . . . and 2) I'll know when I am starting to make progress when . . ." Again, the format of two specific boxes for each topic was designed to call for specific answers.

To be upfront about the critical criteria for good decision-making, the Starting and Check Point Profile pages offered a sidebar reminder of moves we had worked with.

> Tip: A reasoned, reflective decision includes
> √   Specific details
> √   Reasons (because . . .)
> √   Rivals (someone might say . . .)
> √   Roadblocks or qualifications (but, maybe, might . . .)
> √   Conditions (if . . . then . . .)

The Check Point Profile

The Check Point starts by inviting an updated Network of Support. Then, to motivate a discussion of some of the same questions asked in the Starting Point, it sketches a scenario that asks:

> Imagine that you are about to have a job interview with a new Supervisor. He or she has read your resume, but what they are really thinking is:
>
> - Is this person going to be a good member of my team?
> - Can she take responsibility? Can he make good decisions?
> - So how can you show that Supervisor what you can do?

The Profile then asks them to respond to the question by thinking of a time they had to make a decision and to then:

1. Describe the problem and the Story-Behind-the-Story.
2. Describe how you made the decision: your options, rivals, and outcomes.
3. Now tell what it shows about YOU!

Appendix 3.2. Asset Analysis Included in the Scholar's Journey Book

The Scholars' individual Journey Book included pre- and post-graphs from the Asset Analysis, plus pie charts based on the Scholar's decision-making statements. The Asset graph below is an example of an aggregated display of the five groups of assets made for each school who participated. These visual displays stimulated discussion for the Scholars and increased the impact for adult readers.

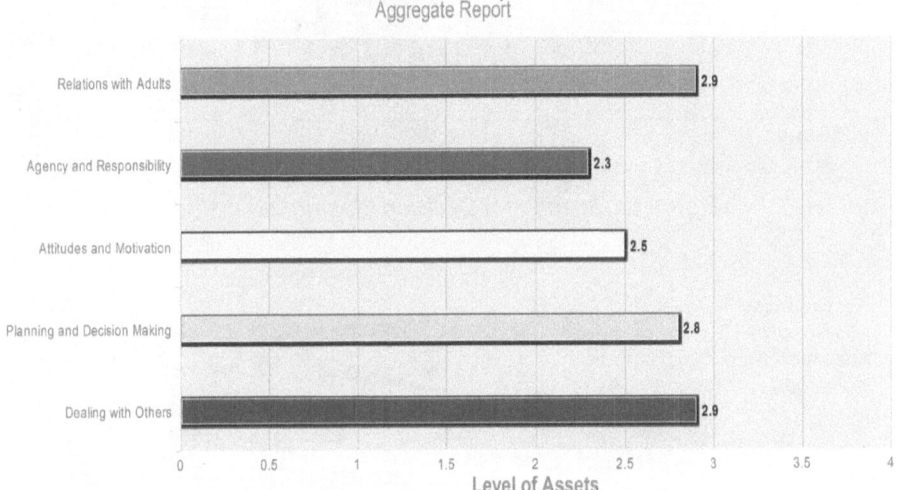

Figure 3.1. Level of assets.

The two pie charts below show the proportion of each type of statement this student was making in their pre-test at the beginning of the program and then six months later. The following reminder box was in the margin of the Profile they were creating.

Remember, a reasoned, reflective decision includes
- Specific details
- Reasons (because...)
- Rivals (someone might say...)
- Roadblocks (but, since, if...then)
- Reflections on your choices

Figures 3.2 and 3.3 show pre- and post-test changes in growth of reflective decision making.

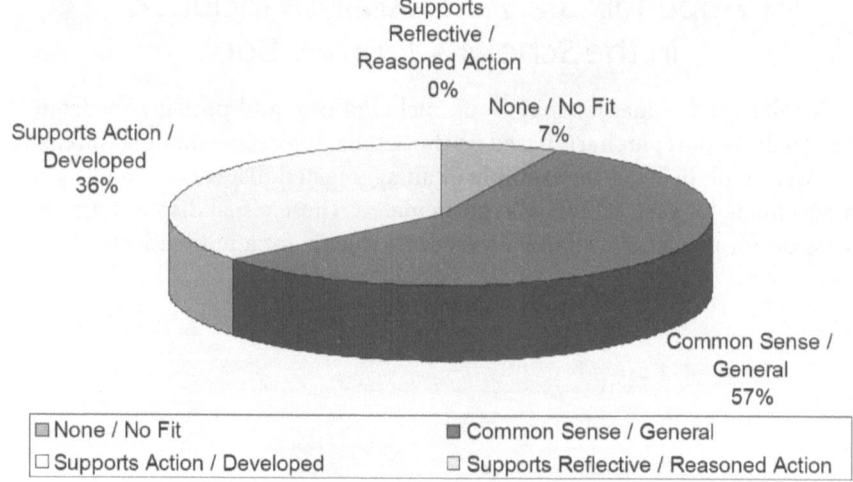

Figure 3.2. Scoring for Decision Making (pre-test)

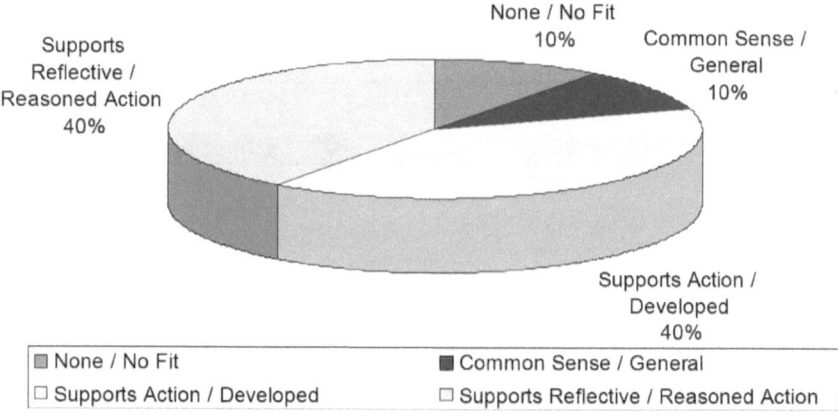

Figure 3.3. Scoring for Decision Making (post-test)

Those results are also accompanied by a table showing them numerically.

Scoring Rubric for Reflective Decision Making	Starting Point	Check Point
Level 0 None/No Fit	7%	10%
Level 1 Common Sense/General	57%	10%
Level 2 Supports Action	36%	40%
Level 3 Supports Reflective Reasoned Action	0%	40%

These figures are unlikely to show simple intellectual development. Rather they reflect these writers' awareness of and ability to use powerful new strategies in a context that called for them.

Chapter 4. Interrogating Hidden Frames as a Path to Change

> As I said, this moment does not mark some decisive victory in gay rights—but it does within *my* sphere. It is a victory that *I* helped create within the sphere in which *I* have power to make a change.
>
> – Justine

The Problem: Interpretative Frames at Work

Social engagement is a powerful teacher that broadens the scope of learning to the way ideas, contexts, other people with their differing traditions, values and goals, interact.[1] It creates that "expansive learning" Yrjö Engeström has described in which more elements of an entire activity system, as well as its conflicts and contradictions, are recognized (Introduction). However, insight needs to pierce the veil in two directions by recognizing not only what is "out there" but also our own silent interpretive process—the assumptions, constructions, omissions—which we bring to creating our own "knowing." And it is engagement with other realities that provides the pushback to let us see what our own internal voices are saying. So this chapter will look at a way writing conjoined with engagement can let us probe and respond to those hidden interpretive frames.

The agenda in education, one that is giving critical, social, and local engagement a visible place in our pedagogy, is calling for a demanding form of praxis as Paulo Freire sees it—a cycle of action and reflection in which theory and practice interact. It is also an intersectional agenda trying to recognize forces that are described so differently in rhetoric and composition, cultural studies, communication, policy, and social movement work. And in this broad interactive space, writing, as Linda Adler-Kassner, Robert Crooks, and Ann Watters put it, "is so much more, . . . [a] strategy that can be used for learning, a way of negotiating identities within and around specific contexts, a representation of ideas, a way of participating in ideologies, a strategy for movement" ("Service-Learning" 318). That may seem like a lot to ask, especially of assigned written work in a college course. The questions here are, "How might socially engaged courses support such a strategic rhetorical art?" and "How can (can?) writing, in particular, create that space in which identity, ideology, and social interaction actually shape one another?"

---

1. This chapter originally appeared in *College Composition and Communication*. Flower, Linda. "Hidden Frames: Writing a Path to Change." *College Composition and Communication*, vol. 73, no. 1, 2021, pp. 27–51. Copyright 2021 by the National Council of Teachers of English. Reprinted with permission.

Our interdisciplinary visions of engagement often vary in their focus, whether it is on ideology, partnerships, rhetorical agency, or social action. However, for writers, one of the critical forces to be reckoned with is the role (for good and for ill) of the interpretive frames we bring to our work. Interpretive frames (as they are described in communication, policy, and psychological studies) are rhetorical, presentational devices constructed to selectively emphasize or hide features of an issue.[2] They let us make quick sense of things, prompting us, for instance, to make snap judgments about the intelligence of students based on their linguistic fluency, or style of arguing, or simply their control of academic discourse (Hull). As social constructs, interpretive frames such as those circulating through our reading and writing can provide a logic that scripts the exercise of power and exclusion. Writing, as a tool for social engagement in education, is often used to critique and challenge the frames that exclude and silence the voices of others. This chapter is about just such interpretive frames—*when these frames are our own*. And how writing—in the form of theory-guided metacognitive analysis—can be an actionable force for change for our students (and ourselves). After exploring some of the options for dealing with these frames, I want to focus on how students in a publicly engaged course translated insight into actions.

Dealing with Cultural Frames

The interrogating gaze of critical discourse has taught us to recognize those whispered voices of culturally created "common sense" and how they shape the social messages buried in our texts, arguments, assumptions, and interpretations. Ideology, one name we give to this amorphous force, supplies us with its "invested patterns of ideas that explain and justify society as it is [which in turn] establishes belief" (Dana Cloud 57). In response, cultural criticism has given us new

---

2. In argument theory, the term "framing" typically refers to a context created to present the problem in a certain light (Benford and Snow). In policy studies, frames are even more action-oriented, providing a "normative-prescriptive story that sets out a problematic policy problem and a course of action to be taken" (Rein and Schoen, qtd. in Fischer 144). As a real workhorse in the face of conflicting frames that socially construct the problem situation, they provide "conceptual coherence, a direction for action, a basis for persuasion and a framework for the collections and analysis of data—order, action, rhetoric and analysis" (Rein and Schoen, qtd. in Fischer 144). In Erving Goffman's sociological account, they go even further to re/frame or rekey a situation to transform what people think is going on in a strip of discourse (8). In psychology, the related notion of schema describes an individual's partially shared mental network of ideas, images, etc., that are learned over time rather than preconstructed (Anderson). In rhetoric, "rhetorical archetypes" such as the Gay Warrior archetype Doug Cloud has documented in military controversies, work as "repetitive, prototypical representations of identity categories that circulate widely and are used to support arguments—the 'stock characters' of rhetorical discourse" ("The Rise" 29). These variations highlight the variety of ways frames can be created and/or used.

conceptual tools to uncover ideology's presence and oppressive effects enacted through interpretive frames.

But a new take on what is missing from such critique comes from Dana Cloud, a self-described socialist, critical rhetorical scholar of political discourse, and practicing working-class activist. She has been a card-carrying member of what she calls "the Culture of Critical Discourse," or CCD. However, her recent work in *Reality Bites* marks a re-orientation to wider public change that this critical discourse, she argues, has still *failed* to enact. One problem is that the tactics of CCD she describes simply can't compete with social doxa—received common sense—as a force for social change. Moreover, this rational, analytical "perspective from which to perform criticism in the service of demystifying power" is itself an elite discourse, addressed to the already-persuaded (5). And most importantly, she argues, it fails to recognize, much less draw upon or value, the perspectives of the people marginalized or oppressed by dominant paradigms. CCD fails to represent the knowledge and stories of marginalized voices as *voices* rather than the *topic* of its critical analysis. And secondly, its rationalized rhetoric of critique simply lacks the power to compel change.

Within rhetoric and composition, one strong response to this problem of representation has been to draw out, prize, and publish the unacknowledged knowledge created in the experience of community partnerships (Goldblatt), community publishing (Parks, "Strategic"), urban teenagers (Flower, "Community Lit"), neighborhood adults (Rousculp), streetwise news writers (Mathieu), nursing aids (Flower, "Negotiating"), Native American storytellers (Cushman), Chicago street gangs (Cintron), community "instructors" (Shah), gay high school teachers (Clifton), or refugees (Long), to name a few. For the college students embedded in such projects, their own intellectual, intercultural, and sociopolitical development is also extended by writing.

Within academic criticism, the related approach Dana Cloud proposes is to refocus that "Culture of Critical Discourse" less on the markers of oppressive ideology (as *we,* of course, perceive them) and more on what is missing, what we overlook: the voices and experience of those people most subjected to the operations of such ideology.

To do so would mean first identifying the interpretive frames that are in play in, say, discussions of immigrants, welfare recipients, or first-generation students. These widely received ideological frames mediate our perception in the shape of "invisible naturalized common sense associated with a *dominant* group's interest" (Dana Cloud 63, emphasis added). Like the more specific constructs or mental schemas studied in psychological research, they are essentially "strategies for handling social truths through filtering for salience and emphasis" (61). That is, they tell us to hone in on what is both relevant (in the context *they* invoke) and important (from *their* perspective). Using interpretive frames is a normal psychological process. However, not all frames have the same ethical standing when they select for what matters, as when, for instance, they frame immigrants as a wave or hoard of uneducated and illegal border crossers seeking to suck up our taxes and live off welfare (although, ironically, they are also assumed to be stealing our jobs). With the help of a corporately controlled media, such interpretive frames, which also tend to serve various political and financial interests, become turned into *doxa*—into common sense.

What Cloud calls for is not simply exposing or naming the pieces of such interpretive frames but, rather, asking: what is left out or covered up; whose voices are ignored or silenced; and what are the lived experiences, the values, the goals of those guest workers, asylum-seekers, and (daring or desperate) border crossers? In contrast to liberals' current obsession with the rhetoric of "fact-checking," Cloud calls for two alternative practices. The first is what she calls "frame-checking," which asks, "*Whose knowledge is it? Who is it by and who is it for? Who is left out?*" (136). Secondly, the goal here is not just "to perform criticism in the service of demystifying power" but also to create "an oppositional 'reality-based' community that can 'bite back'" (8). She calls, that is, for a form of "rhetorical realism" that can direct and incite action.

Dana Cloud's explicit call for an altered stance to social justice would revise both the academic discourse of critique and the public, political rhetoric of "fact-checking" by drawing instead on the powerful rhetoric of what she calls the "Big Five" strategies: Narrative, Myth, Embodiment, Affect, and Spectacle. Although all these are often associated with effectively deceptive manipulation (as most any rhetorical strategy can be), the ethical test Cloud proposes is their "fidelity or faithfulness . . . to the interests and goals of the people being addressed by and constituted in them" (161). In other words, the Big Five strategies are ethical to the extent that *the voices/ concerns/interests of the marginalized are accurately represented*. Cloud, then, maps out an important path to social change based on stimulating mass social movement with tools that can scale up circulation in all sorts of mass media.

This publicly performative perspective, however, raises a real challenge for justice-oriented rhetoric and writing teachers: how do you translate the conceptual analysis of a problematic practice into action and change? Moreover, what do you do when a given practice may be marginalizing others without anyone's real intent to do so? In particular, what do we do *when that frame or practice is unconsciously our own*? Like Cloud, this chapter seeks ways to deal with these uninterrogated frames that mediate everyday interpretation. But it chooses to work at the other, individual end of the spectrum, where teachers not only probe our own frames but, in this case, help students do the same. To see what this individualized path does and doesn't offer, I want to put it briefly in context of other contemporary choices by asking: who or what is being diminished by these frames, to whom is this argument addressed, and what sort of rhetorical response, using what discourse, is being proposed?

Dana Cloud, for instance, has studied the way whistleblowers have been framed, to different effects, as heroes, traitors, or queer; or how Planned Parenthood providers are represented by the competing frames of feminism, medical care, legalism, and religious dogmatism. Cloud is speaking to colleagues and activists in the language of cultural theory, but she is calling progressives to turn the Discourse of Cultural Critique and fact-checking into a much more persuasive rhetoric. Designed for the unpersuaded general public, her approach is working subversively, you might say, to draw them into thinking with a *new* interpretive frame. We are her allies, just in need of a better discourse tool.

A concrete instance of what this means turns up in disability studies, in which the frame of normalcy "marks disabled people as 'different' yet simultaneously demands conformity to social and material environments designed primarily for and by 'normal' bodies" (Glavin, Rhetoric). What Mary Glavin's grounded work with actual families goes on to show is that the normalcy frame conceals the rhetorical labor through which both "normal" and "difference" are constructed and perceived. That is, "the emergent, iterative, risk-ridden rhetorical labor of understanding and representing oneself in contested spaces.... where representing a "normal" self is also an agentive act, similarly shaped by networks of individual and structural relationships" (Reframing).

Dealing with Identity Frames

Uninterrogated frames may also be working closer to home. For instance, college can be a place where students can discover who they are or develop a fresh identity. It also opens its closet to a set of well-defined roles complete with all its defining garments you are asked to step into. Though once you don its hat and boots you will feel the pressure to keep them on. Identity frames that dictate choices and actions may be surprisingly insidious. A rural Appalachian student comes up to a high profile competitive urban university and the identity package (hillbilly, redneck, backwards (or underprepared, first generation in academic lingo)) is waiting at their dorm door. If you can't fit into a new costume (i.e., walk, talk, act like a prospective engineer, computer scientist, or even a historian or professional designer) your capabilities, intelligence and even value as a potential class team member will be devalued. And with this suddenly diminished sense of power, you might even buy into some of that assessment yourself.

Amanda Tennant's long-term study of this expectation showed, however, that some students place a high value on their Appalachian identity, with its deeply held values for family and loyalty in a working-class community—an identity they don't want to give up ("Rhetorical College Experience"). But holding onto that old identity frame would come at a cost. In the studies Tennant reviews, power among marginalized communities is often theorized as the ability to navigate the conflicting pressures to pass as members of the dominant, succeed academically, fit in and be accepted socially, while on the other hand, to maintain and honor connections to their backgrounds or group, and critique and resist their marginalization. Yet these pressures are frequently at odd with one another; when one type of power is gained, another is lost.

In this case the identity some students brought with them did not actually stay hidden. However, they crafted a remarkable alternative way to gain power with what Tennant calls *rhetorical (in)visibility*. That is, they undertook the first step of strategic self-reflection to discover which markers were "tellable" in public discourse ("mountaineer talk" is fine) and which (your firearms and "cricks") were not. Taking the next step, to weigh the risk and rewards of these markers in terms of power, allowed them to turn (in)visibility into a strategic rhetorical choice. For instance, students found they could carefully distance themselves from the "untellable" even as they maintained connections to home. Or they would transform Appalachian identity into a marker of diversity. In their writing they learned to draw on the rhetorical power of experiential knowledge, but do so in ways that that readers would not recognize it as an "Appalachian" experience (681). Here is a case where self-reflection let students rise to a conscious awareness of the potential for power tied each of these identify frames. And by crafting an effective rhetorical strategy, to avoid being co-opted by either one.

Nine years later when Tennant returned to interview these graduates, she found they were still quite aware of their strategies for *rhetorical (in)visibility* and even critical of some of their older ones. However, two who had already achieved well-paying jobs on the West Coast, had moved back home to Appalachia, by choice! Ben has translated what is called the Appalachian black hole (escape) narrative into a new frame: the pressure to return home driven by family and values. Their old college friends, who couldn't understand why, kept pressuring them to "get the heck out of there" and go where the money was. But these graduates' reasons speak to the direct rejection of a frame they knew so well: the objective of a college education is to gain wealth and status, that is, get out of Appalachia, abandon that identity, and make money. As Tennant puts it, "Ben resists the assumption that he has failed to live up the expectations for exceptional Appalachians who escape their home region to achieve success and wealth on the West Coast." Instead, Ben and April have come to "frame a narrative of success in terms of place" and its ability to foster "experiential knowledge, [defined as] exposure to the natural world and strong family connections" (*Rhetorical Cultural Experience*). This has become an inspiring study of "reframing."

Unfortunately, some identity frames, such as the role of being a social advocate, come with an almost obligatory script: taking an assertive, even aggressive personal and rhetorical stance may seem a given. People become advocates for a cause because they care or are even passionate about making change. And when the issue involves race or sex or cultural identity they may do so because their own personhood is at stake. As a frame, advocacy dictates both one's role and rhetorical stance—and writers typically expect or demand that readers take their trademark stance.

But in *Arguing Identity and Human Rights,* Doug Cloud opens a new and powerful path as he explores the presence, benefits, and limitations that alternative often competing models of argument and advocacy can give us. What are the tradeoffs of downplaying versus asserting difference or agency, of responding to clichés or asserting a theoretical stance? Building on his subtitle, *Among Rival Options*, this scholarly exploration is uniquely engaging because it is about *choice*, including his own history. For example, in the 1980s Larry Kramer (founder of ACT UP) went after not only the homophobes and government institutions ignoring AIDS, but gay college students themselves ("queer kids") like Cloud. Stridently arguing they weren't "angry enough" Kramer told them that a cool, calm, rational tone (that universal standard of good communication) was no more than a capitulation to white supremacy. Advocacy was attack, and writers should use their own discomfort in order to forcibly create it in others. Looking back, Cloud sees that rival options were not in this identity guide.

> It's easy to see how a young person could read his words and, without a competing narrative, come to think that good activists are angry activists. But I don't want to be an angry activist. I've already done that, and although it was completely appropriate to my situation at the time, it took a terrible toll on me. Today, I choose to go a different way, though the actual choice has unfolded over years. (142)

The issue here is *choice* and how identity frames not only silently interpret your appropriate role, but close down some powerful options.

> For me, a problem-solving state is much more effective. I do my best work when I focus on the options at hand and their probable outcomes, rather than dwell on the moral urgency of combatting White supremacy, of which I am already convinced. This mindset pushes me beyond discomfort, and helps me ask action-oriented questions like these.... (144)

This inquiry into *choice* can be one of the most powerful strategies a rhetorician has.

Dealing with Educational Frames

By contrast, a recent statement from the Conference on College Composition and Communication (CCCC) issues a proclamation, explicitly focused on racism, addressed to academics not as fellow activists but as the locus of the problem. Its very title, "This Ain't Another Statement! This is a <u>DEMAND</u> for Black Linguistic Justice," challenges the assumption that the white, socially constructed norms of "academic language" and "standard English" are desirable standard and demands "widespread systemic change" in our curricula, our discourse, and our commitments as teachers (2020). A direct descendent of the rhetoric of Black Lives Matter and the anti-Black violence movement, it takes its forcefully assertive style into the quiescent space of our classrooms and journals. Disinterested in our good intentions or history of merely principled, supportive "statements," it demands a change in practice. Positioning white readers as the outsiders, speaking, you might say, more "at" than "to" a white us, it jars us into consciousness. The effect of this shift from Doug Cloud's collegial, doable argument to one clearly implicating the reader in the problem has a parallel described in James Cone's classic *Martin & Malcolm & America: A Dream or a Nightmare*. As he sees it, the shockingly radical demands of Malcolm X made previously resistant people turn to Martin Luther King as a welcome model of moderation.

As part of the contemporary academic discussion of racism, this DEMAND is an institutionally embedded statement. In choosing to take an adversarial rhetorical style with its own National Council of Teachers of English constituency, it throws some of the other options in this conversation into relief. One could, for instance, choose to *theorize* anti-racism in broad generalities, urging us to critique our own "humanist" assumptions (Boyle). Other approaches *describe* ways it turns up in language (Bosmajian; Villanueva) or *uncover* forms of microaggression or color-blind racism (Bonilla-Silva). Whether the focus is on our own or public frames, what unites these approaches is their focus on race.

Another set of discourses, more clearly focused on educational frames, speak directly to teachers and theorists, addressing them as colleagues and people of good will—who are often trapped in the doxa of education and its unexamined, marginalizing frames. These contemporary voices may draw on Paulo Freire or Antonio Gramsci, but they locate the problem right in our own classroom practice. In *AntiRacist Writing Assessment Ecologies*, Asao Inoue argues that we are "missing important opportunities to interrogate the dominant discourse as normative or interrogating the hegemonic ways of evaluating texts in classrooms" (19). If we talk about the rhetorical demands of a text with the stock phrases of evaluation (e.g., unity, details, development, and organization), "how will [students] negotiate the ways that any 'text is evaluated' against a dominant white discourse?" (19). However, in place of direct classroom interrogation of that form of hegemony, he asserts that the problem is *assessment itself.*

Inoue sees his larger social/political purpose as challenging "White habitus reinforced," as he says, "by other discourses of empiricism: objectivity, neutrality, hyper individualism, unsentimental, detached discussion, and a Cartesian *Cogito*" (112). But in his own highly diverse classes of students who have had those dominant (racist) criteria used to dismiss and devalue them as writers, his response is to replace the standard processes of evaluating writing with student dialogues in which the class itself negotiates and develops the criteria for an effectual text. Individual grades, then, are based primarily on measurements of the "labor" the writer puts into developing, discussing, and creating that text. This response is designed to make those (often internalized) frames that define one's identity as a writer simply irrelevant. And the measure of success is seeing students reflect on the remarkable discovery that they had choice within rubrics, such as organization, and that disagreement was acceptable (e.g., did the thesis really *have* to be up front, and apparently you *could* use "I"). And in some cases, this new confidence even translated into the motivation to learn some of those "standard" features.

Like Inoue, I wanted the students in my publicly engaged courses described in previous chapters to question the interpretative frames they use to evaluate their writing and to engage with others. In Inoue's case, the competing frames students needed to recognize were those of upper level "theme writing" and a formally "well-developed essay." However, in my community-engaged courses, success was more likely to depend on rhetorical invention, demanding both discovery and change. And the assessment frame in the headlights here was application: are you able to apply your learning to a new rhetorical situation, to take it beyond theory or generalized concepts into situated practice?

Using the Lens of Frame Analysis

A final new educational alternative to consider would not just critique frames but change them. Rather than focus on a given problematic frame used by others, such as "Standard English," it would put the frame in context, in an expanded universe—in an ecological frame. The metaphor of rhetorical *ecologies*, as Nathaniel Rivers and Ryan Weber use it, replaces the tidy image of a communication triangle with an expanded rhetorical universe of social action through public rhetoric. Using the Montgomery Bus Boycott, they model an ecological analysis that translates this rhetorical situation into a dynamic, intensely networked rhetorical and material landscape. Their analysis turns a short story of Rosa Parks' courageous action and Martin Luther King's leadership into a fully staged drama sustained by a "diverse environment of mundane, concatenated texts and counter-rhetorics," which includes not only letters and speeches but "newsletters, internal memos, proposals, strategy documents, images of protests and the spaces . . . that shaped and were shaped by rhetorical activity" (196–97). Without the energy that circulated through this network, the Bus Boycott's 381-day joint effort would never have been sustained. When students take this ecological orientation in a public rhetoric class project, it becomes a tool that transforms their "background" research—giving it "an expanded scope that views rhetorical action as emergent and enacted through a complex ecology of texts, writers, readers, institutions, objects and history" (188). Like Dana Cloud's frame checking, it zooms out, embedding us in a larger cast of characters.

This brief review of approaches to the work and the danger of frames suggests the rich diversity of our field's own interpretative frames for dealing with *representations that marginalize* others. And because the success of substantive *social* change (i.e., not just political reorganization) is never complete and rarely stable, I believe we need to work on multiple fronts and down all the paths we can muster. This study of hidden frames will describe yet another way to instantiate change, though not only a public voice but also by supporting individual, self-conscious action in everyday social interactions with family, colleagues, a classroom or community. The goal of this alternative rhetoric was to help students create a local path to action, starting with a theory-guided investigation of frames at work in their own, often-unquestioned practice. In doing so, students soon began to notice the previously undetected consequences of their actions at work within the ecology of a family, an institution, a class, within policy documents and class plans, in subsequent lectures, formal meetings, and uneasy conversations with peers, as well as in some unanticipated effects on a wide body of students.

Finally, frame analysis can be turned into a detailed yet coherent way to present what Alex Helberg calls a "contextually aware strategic communication plan." His study of two ideologically and locally competing food donating programs—one doing their civic duty to combat waste, the other with an anarchist agenda to combat poverty based on political capitalism. To help activists understand what they are facing, he created a brief guide for "How to Frame a Complex Systemic Issue." Designed as a table, it names three key moves we can make to develop a coherent set of *problem/solution framing* strategies, a set of *conceptual metaphors* to help simplify the complexity of the issue, and a coherent and discrete set of *identities* & roles for your prospective participants. In the Guide each frame is explored with Generative Questions and Examples, such as "Who has the ability to take action on behalf of this issue?" and What are their "identity markers?" The examples allow a close comparison of the stance of the (well-off) citizen "Food Rescue Heroes" to that of the Food Not Bombs anarchist group dedicated to "fighting the greed and power" of institutions and business. His use of a data-based frame analysis created an insightful guide to dealing with a complex, politically charged situation with a strategic community plan.

The Metacognitive Path: From Analysis to Reflection to Actionable Critical Consciousness

Like the critical and rhetorical approaches noted earlier, social movement studies map a road to action, with a difference. In Robert D. Benford and David A. Snow's extraordinary review of that research, what really matters is the *transformation* and *use* of interpretive frames. In this action-oriented context, frames are not merely the hidden perpetrators of exclusion scripted by interest and power; they are the rhetorical engine driving social action. Frames interpret the "world out there" (such as the detention of *illegal immigrants*, or alternatively, of *asylum seekers*) in order to "render events or occurrences meaningful" (614). More to the point, they are not given but must be constructed to work as what Benford and Snow call "collective action frames" (611). Here, "framing" is a verb that "denotes an active, processual phenomenon that implies agency and contention at the level of reality construction" (614). As Frank Fischer's useful work in *Reframing Public Policy* demonstrates, framing (and/or "reframing") some "reality" can not only challenge existing ways of making sense of things but do the cognitive work of supplying us not only with a problem definition and diagnosis of the cause, but a map for action, and the grounds for persuasion (144).

I raise this positive perspective on how frames *can work* to put our metacognitive path in perspective. We could read Dana Cloud and Benford and Snow as each sketching two necessary but different paths to change. Cloud's *Culture of Critical Discourse* produces a language of critique designed to reveal power and promote awareness and critical consciousness. Her expansion of this discourse would enlarge its agenda to include marginalized voices and invent a more aggressive (and effective) rhetoric to put this critique into wide circulation. Benford and Snow's social movement agenda, on the other hand, comes to life in the highly interactive, constructive context of creating and transforming frames. Their desired outcome is a motivating "collective action" frame. The work of metacognitive inquiry described here lies somewhere between critique and collective action. Its path is routed through an analysis of the (typically unexamined) exclusionary interpretive frames operating within our own experience. The outcome, when initiated in an educational setting, can be a negotiated one that recognizes conflicted and missing knowledge, a probing discussion with others, or the foundation for a working theory that attempts to transform that frame into a more inclusive practice.

From my particular perspective, in problem-solving cognition and actionable rhetoric as well as community writing, the problem looks like this: how do we, each of us, open up a live circuit that leads from critique to the grounded, internal, cognitive work of interpretation that guides our sometimes-unconsidered responses to problematic situations? This is the site of *situated cognition*, the place where ideas are operationalized in *interactions* with others. It is at this dynamic intersection of experience and metacognitive inquiry that we can see a path, not just to changing others but also ourselves—and to helping students likewise carry out their own education for engagement.

The actionable critical consciousness in the cases sketched below can be triggered by ordinary experience when reality does indeed "bite," when it directly challenges a familiar interpretive frame and pushes us to a *meta*cognitive awareness of the friction between expectation and experience. That friction can push us to thinking about our own thinking when, for instance, we suddenly realize that what we perceived as a student's "natural" accidental "slip" into "ungrammatical" Black English was, in fact, not only intentional but was a precise and effective linguistic choice. (So where did *that* response come from? Why? How could it play out?) Admittedly, acknowledging internal conflicts and contradictions is not our mental strong suit as humans. From a psychological perspective, when familiar schemas are violated, our first response is to ignore the anomaly or simply "assimilate" it somehow into our schema-guided expectations. We can compartmentalize and hold competing interpretations, beliefs, and values quite comfortably, as it turns out. Actually altering, or what is called "accommodating," the schema itself is another matter. That may require a real "confrontation with difficulties of one's current schema" (Anderson 429). Moreover, rising to metacognitive awareness of a conflict is a *choice*, a move from automatic or merely tacit interpretation to a more conscious level of reflective problem solving.³ As we will see in the examples below, this choice is often affectively triggered, but actionable consciousness for change typically calls for more extended metacognitive work—in which writing can be a transformative force.⁴

Writing toward a more *actionable* critical consciousness will also need to take a student beyond many of our classroom practices for reflection on their writing.⁵ In the following cases, we see how a class can ramp up the familiar process of reflection-prompted-by-experience into building a working theory with four moves. The process starts by using theoretically grounded *critical concepts* to then guide a *rhetorical analysis* of one's own interpretations and actions, in order to then create an even more sophisticated *metacognitive analysis* of those actions. The final, fourth move is the work of praxis: using the insights of this meta-analysis to develop a *working theory* for going forward.⁶ As an educational practice, the path starts with students' study of rich theoretical concepts, such as (in the following cases) rhetoric's conception of frame analysis, psychology's

---

3. Extensively studied in educational psychology, the term "metacognition" can refer to a tacit control process (such as monitoring a failure in comprehension that prompts us to reread a phrase), or to a conscious access and control of one's own knowledge or reflective understanding—an awareness educational researchers Ann Brown and Annemarie Palincsar see as a flexible hallmark of higher intelligence. Others reserve the term for awareness of one's own action *and* the ability to *articulate* that awareness (Paris and Winograd). The data for this study comes from that final, more powerful level of articulated metaknowledge.

4. In a study of college students' reflections on their thinking and discoveries in a traditional class, I found their series of written insights displayed strong three-way links between their affect or emotions, the context of writing, and their cognition, including goals, options, and strategies. Even more significant, rising to this level of awareness worked as a critical prompt to the construction of "negotiated meaning"—a sophisticated representation that engages with multiple voices as well as conflict (Flower, *Construction*).

5. Reflection has myriad forms and purposes shaped by what is reflected upon: our own writing or a teacher's comments (in composition studies); formative memories (in therapy); perplexing experiences (in social interaction); and prior knowledge (in transfer). For a useful introduction to classroom research and practice, see Kathleen Yancy's *A Rhetoric of Reflection* and the review of research in Chapter 2.

6. Here I use the phrase "metacognitive reflection and analysis" to recognize a level of metacognition that is a self-conscious, intentional attention to our own thinking and to articulating the work of cognition. Because the mind and its mental notebooks speak so rapidly in multiple languages (images, propositional representations, and prose) and are inseparable from affect, bringing this to conscious attention (much less in an articulate version) is no small task (Flower and Hayes, "Images"). But the metacognitive process of thinking about our thinking can let us bring to light and up for review how our often unanalyzed, and even unrecognized ways of knowing are at work in our minds.

mental models, or leadership's distinction between technical problems and adaptive challenges.

Drawing on complex concepts like these lets students map out a closely observed analysis of some unrecognized interpretive frames at work in their own experience. They are creating a guided, case-in-point analysis. Their end in view, however, is not merely a structured academic analysis but a working theory of actionable critical consciousness—a foundation for social engagement. In taking on this combination of intellectually complex rhetorical inquiry and an intentional, problem-oriented, personal metacognitive analysis, writers will probably have to construct a new negotiated meaning—one that recognizes and attempts to deal with some of the conflicts, contradictions, and alternatives they have exposed. It is this expanded construct that provides the basis for a *working theory*. By *theory*, I mean a critical, conceptual construct that remains open to evidence and reinterpretation and is at the same time a guide to choice and action: a theory that supports *work*.[7]

This chapter will explore two versions of this self-initiated, individual path. One is the familiar act of a *reflection* triggered by experience. The other is a more intentional effort designed to confront interpretive frames—a process I will describe as a *theory-guided metacognitive analysis*. In both cases, the process will be complicated by the fact that exclusionary frameworks are often embedded in good intentions.

Case 1: When Experience Bites Back

We can all relate to that uncomfortable moment when the resistant reality of experience forced us to confront one of our own (underexamined) interpretive frames. Liz, a white, first-time mentor at the Community Literacy Center was working hard in her literature courses to become an insider to the Culture of Critical Discourse. Her plan for mentoring 14-year-old, inner-city Chaz was, as she put it, "helping him to develop a consciousness that might not have been there. He wants to be a professional football player. I challenge that. He's a little guy, you know. I ask him to analyze this cultural thing—football, which I don't think is too

---

7. The concept of rising to negotiated meaning grows out of studies tracking the thinking of both experienced and inexperienced writers and the differences in how they respond to internal conflict as they are writing. While novices just roll on, ignoring tangled or competing voices, the experienced writers stop to listen, attempting to create a meaning (an idea, argument, a sentence) that responds to those voices (Flower, *Construction*). The notion of working theories, on the other hand, comes from observing the outcomes of intercultural Community Think Tanks. The actively negotiated, documented meaning these different groups produced was not simply a set of claims or conclusions. Rather it was a usable, action-oriented but tentative interpretation (a theory in the form of a revisable hypothesis) designed to address a real situation, that is, to work (Flower, "Difference-Driven Inquiry").

much to ask of someone at this age level" (Flower, *Community Literacy* 118). But Chaz wasn't the only skinny Black kid who talked this line. Did Liz understand what this sort of aspirational boast actually *meant* for him? Was it an identity assertion to her, just a part of teen talk, or . . . ? Did she think to find out?

Another mentor named Dianna, an elegant, West Coast, middle-class African American senior, seemed to be taking umbrage at our discussion about "Black English." I had been sharing with the teens the influential linguistic research of William Labov (arguing for Black English as a legitimate dialect in the face of the public schools' choice to penalize it) and Geneva Smitherman's examples in *Talkin' and Testifyin': The Language of Black America*. My "socially engaged teacher" interpretive frame prompted me first to describe/clarify some of the distinctions in grammar and diction between "standard written" and "Black" English. Secondly, in order to help these teenage writers consider the linguistic *choices* open to them, I intended to challenge the assumption many held that "this is just my *bad* English." Even if one option was expected in school, here they were writing from and about urban teenage life. Their texts would be published and circulated in a newsletter they titled *Risk and Respect*, and some would be translated into performance and dialogue with the audience at the project's closing Community Conversation. For many teenage writers, giving this formal standing to Black English had been a liberating new concept, letting them choose to use (and edit for) standard written English and switch to their own dialect for dramatic and rhetorical effect. But to my surprise, my educated college student was clearly resisting this solidly supported academic perspective, even angry that I was promoting it.

Perplexed, I asked to have lunch with Dianna (and her brother, who was in town) at a nearby café to talk it over. It was only then that I discovered, first, that she could not herself speak the "Black English" of our urban teenagers—something she did not wish to reveal to them. And secondly, in her interpretive frame (for what *I saw* as a liberating conception of the linguistic legitimacy and power of a dialect spoken by many African Americans), she saw a threat that questioned her own *Black* identity by equating the two. In short, there was a legitimate conflict that had never crossed my mind, even as I, the professor, was clearly marginalizing her in the way I presented "Black English" as an uncontextualized, normative aspect of race: as academic commonsense. "Of course she can speak Black English . . . she's Black."

In this case, it took a direct conversation to elicit this conflict with my interpretive frame and all that my well-intentioned philosophy had not dreamed of. However, that was hardly enough; then came the metacognitive work of figuring out how to acknowledge this more complex reality and still help other writers question why they asserted that their rich linguistic repertoire was simply "bad English." It is one thing to point out the marginalizing frames at work in the discourse of others. It is another, first, to recognize how your own liberal, progressive, often-academic frames are blinding you to the reality of other peoples' lives; and secondly, to figure out how to act differently. Recognizing your own automatic interpretive processes is the first step in this metacognitive inquiry, but it is not enough merely to recognize the phenomenon. The challenge is figuring out the working theory—how to alter them.

So what follows consciousness? Growing up in Wichita, Kansas, where it seemed to my seven-year-old self that the Black people I rarely saw all lived in a rather forbidding territory across town. My stereotypes stayed intact upon moving to a small town in Iowa, which as far as I ever knew, included only two Black families and two Jewish families. In college, my sorority even had to fight the national organization to admit the one Black woman on campus at the time. That meant, beyond a religious commitment to justice and equality, that I had a limited experiential basis from which to directly challenge some of the negative images of Black people woven into the public imagination during this civil rights era.

So when, as an adult, I began to build strong intercultural connections in one of Pittsburgh's troubled and vibrant urban neighborhoods through the Community Literacy Center, all that implicitly learned ideological education and ignorance and baggage did not simply disappear. Walking down an urban street, my well-learned racial and class-based interpretive stereotypes could be automatically triggered by an approaching Black teenager in a hoodie, slowly crossing the street, conspicuously ignoring traffic, with his trousers apparently held up only by a miracle. That implicit racist ideological trigger is still there. Yet in the next nanosecond, a metacognitive awareness of that frame and its alternatives also kicks in. And I can draw on alternative interpretations learned from teens themselves in which hoodies, for example, signaled teen fashion on the Northside, not gang membership—and my awareness that police couldn't tell the difference. With that interpretation comes an alternative action learned in that culture: when you meet a Black person on the sidewalk, you smile or merely nod, a simple gesture merely meant to acknowledge presence. It's a move that is common in our Black community, whether you know the person or not. Black people give you a comfortable nod back. After all these years, that act is still a conscious, pleasurable metacognitive choice.

In these everyday examples, our experience, interactions, and face-to-face inquiry can draw us all into the reflective awareness that affects behavior. I use my own experience here to be clear that I (and I expect other educators) are not exempt. So we design our socially engaged courses with various action agendas that will take students beyond critical deconstruction of media and culture and into interpersonal encounters. The interaction itself is a teacher.

There are, however, less obvious forms of marginalization. Having drunk from the cup of our culture, we carry its internalized interpretive triggers with us. Their unbidden messages do not, however, *have* to dictate how we think or act when we can confront them with an articulated alternative—the kind of interpretation that is uniquely enabled by written inquiry. This account is motivated by what I learned observing students using writing to translate theory into a personal frame analysis with practical consequences. Let me put this cycle of metacognitive inquiry in context.

Case 2: Intentional Metacognitive Analysis

This case will illustrate an alternative, self-conscious reflective practice rooted in a *theory-based* examination of interpretative frames. Its structured metacognitive analysis unpacks exclusionary assumptions as a guide to imagining a new working theory. Writers Josh and Justine were part of that socially engaged rhetoric course called Leadership, Dialogue, and Change (Chapter 2, Case 2). Beginning with extensive reading in intercultural theories of leadership and dialogue, it led to a Community Think Tank around the problem of learning about and using self-advocacy in which they documented different perspectives and the results of their cross-hierarchy, problem-focused series of roundtable dialogues.[8] The course's final individual paper was a four-page "personal inquiry" assignment that asked students to consider how they had applied their personal discoveries from the course in their own lives. Their writing suggests the distinctive kind of insight a theory-prompted, metacognitive analysis can create.

When Analysis Calls for Transformation

One of the most influential tools for rhetorical analysis we studied was a framework for leadership in public conflicts, developed by Ronald Heifetz at Harvard's Kennedy School for Government. In *Leadership without Easy Answers,* Heifetz develops his theory of adaptive leadership through a series of fascinating case studies, making a distinction between "technical problems" (ones we already know how to manage) and "adaptive problems" that demand a new understanding. Such a dilemma faced the Environmental Protection Agency in 1983. Should they enforce regulations and in effect force the closure of an aging, out-of-compliance, arsenic-spewing American Smelting and Refining Company (ASARCO) plant outside Tacoma, WA—and in the process destroy a three-generation local economy? The pressure on EPA head William Ruckelshaus—from both labor and environmentalists—was to use his authority to treat it as a "technical problem" and to act decisively in "their" (differing) interests. Heifetz's model of leadership in such a case is a dramatic departure from the stereotype of the charismatic leader, whose acts of forceful decision-making and persuasion turn others into

---

8. This particular Think Tank was prompted by questions about students' problematic experiences in learning and using self-advocacy. Using the Think Tank's standard research and critical incident interviews with students, faculty, and staff, developing a Briefing Book designed for a diverse set of participants at roundtable, problem-solving discussions, they documented and published them as the Think Tank Findings on Self Advocacy (Bennett et al.; Flower, "Difference-Driven Inquiry").

followers. Heifetz describes an even more demanding rhetorical act in which leaders must work to draw a community (a family, an organization, and a public) to face an "adaptive" problem. Unlike the more comfortable "technical" ones, for which one already has expertise, standard tools, or practices in hand, adaptive problems come with a price. They are likely to require that members of a divided community not only learn new things but, in all probability, also reexamine and revise some of their own assumptions and values in the context of others.

Is the choice in Tacoma simply "to close or not to close?" Whose interests should be left out: a third-generation, breadwinning worker who loses a sustaining job; a resident of the surrounding area who receives no profit from this industry except its arsenic-laden, cancer-causing air currents; or the company and its stockholders? When Heifetz's model "gives the problem back" to the citizens, months of simply oppositional debate are morphed, with the help of Ruckelshaus's team, into long series of public discussions in which the different stakeholders begin to reframe the issue into how to both protect their air and children and also create a path to work. This was a problem they, in fact, eventually solved. The challenge here is not to "win" but to recognize the partiality of your own frame and the reasonable motives behind those of others—and to then create a new "adaptive" frame and a way to carry it out.

What We Observed

As a good illustration of the "public turn," this case illustrates a working theory in action. Josh entered the Leadership, Dialogue, and Change class with significant leadership experience. A junior in Information Systems, he was a member of the University Leadership Consultants, a student group which offers consultations with campus organizations "suffering [as he put it] from leadership related issues"—in this case, a squash club suffering from low member turnout at events. The consulting group had a well-developed frame for reading these "issues," tied to a very efficient two- to three-week process in which they would, "internally, decide on what was best for the organization and perform a training or (standard) workshop." Unfortunately, as Josh began to recognize, "the issue the organization was suffering with was rarely, if ever, solved." Though "an incredibly speedy process, it . . . resulted in unsatisfactory or meaningless results."

When it came time to write his final "applied theory" paper, Josh had already experienced an extended cycle of inquiry, documenting and dramatizing marginalized perspectives as part of a diverse Think Tank deliberation. Were he to write a standard "applied theory" paper, he could have made excellent use of Heifetz's leadership theory to analyze the problematic practices of the consultants. However, this paper was asking for a more direct application to one's own practices and the thinking behind them, in order to make personal use of what had been learned.

Starting with Heifetz's concept of engaging a community in dialogue, Josh describes beginning to see limitations in his own, quite self-conscious model of "servant-leadership," which he says he had advocated "since high school . . . I fell into the trap of a technical leader who was more focused on solving tasks." This would matter when it turned out that the squash club's "low-turnout" problem wasn't with the no-shows or the organization's advertising at all, but instead with a dysfunctional leadership team, which never worked as a group to figure out what events new members might actually want to come to.

Josh's text goes on to articulate the outcome of changing his "perspective on leadership to an expanded value-based one." And perhaps more usefully, he begins to build an operational analysis of what this means. "Instead of asking myself the question 'what needs doing?' I now ask 'why does this need doing? What is the real problem here? How can I engage the community?'" This self-analysis then had a public outcome when his University Leadership Consultants changed their process. Sitting down with the squash club, the consultants replaced their "cookie cutter workshop" with probing questions about the club's operations and hinderances. They soon discovered that the club's actual barrier to growth was that it had no idea of how to get financial help to renovate the old courts—a problem which the consultants' "typical recruit, retrain, and grow presentation" could not have identified, much less addressed.

Some problems, however, are not so easily resolved by following a thoughtful, even persuasive, theory-guided revision of one's framework. Josh had also been a student member of the university committee that had just radically shortened the "add/drop" period for classes. But as it went into action, he now found himself the representative to his peers of a widely unpopular mandate. His account of this unresolved problem is an even better example of how a written, metacognitive analysis can pull out some of the assumptions the committee's interpretive frame brought with it—and whose needs it excluded. The committee's ostensible, well-intentioned policy was focused not merely on filling classes sooner (an institutional priority) but on relieving the very real stress caused by the increasing practice of students overloading their schedules and then only dropping a class when the damage to their learning or health had already been done. But then, as Josh writes, "With Heifetz in mind, I wonder if that [interpretation] was actually the case?"

In his new analysis, Josh considers how the decision he supported "reeks of an authority figure . . . attempting to 'protect' its community without allowing the community to fully engage and grapple with its issues." By focusing on a symptom (late drops) rather than the problem, the new policy forces students who can't drop to suffer through classes they should have quit. Moreover, the policy fails to deal with other, real sources of stress. But when you are in a leader's chair, you must often go beyond critique. Josh's analysis not only raised new voices but significantly shifted the frame to the broader issue of stress itself. Questioning whether the committee's solution had indeed located a real cause of stress led him to form an inventive working theory for a more inclusive dialogue. His analysis ends by sketching an intriguing plan for a campus-wide contest eliciting solutions to stress, which would lead to a university-vetted proposal to be discussed in campus forums. Using the theoretical lens of leadership based on inclusive dialogue, Josh's metacognitive analysis let him unpack and evaluate the elements of his own interpretive frame, what he calls "the rhetorical moves I didn't even know I was making!" In taking the next step beyond retrospective reflection, he initiated a constructive act that translated understanding into everyday action and began to develop a working theory which, as he says, "I want to bring to the [university] committee."

It is important to recognize that in the messy and conflict-prone sites of community engagement, complete "success" is rarely the norm and our interpretive frames for dealing with failure can play a large role in what we do next. Amanda Tennant, Carolyn Commer, and Mary Glavan give us a provocative rhetorical analysis of "transformative failure" in community-based projects, where a failure frame can block our ability to see the trade-offs at work in what we did and didn't achieve. When the young Appalachian girls in Tennant's summer program failed to produce the polished but stereotypical "mountain girl" narratives the program's PR-focused director and donors expected, the failure frame cast its shadow on the girls and mentors but was felt most personally by Tennant, the leader of this particular project. However, the authors use their three cases of felt failure to demonstrate the power of a frame-probing "reflective heuristic." By using strategies such as seeking rival hypotheses to interrogate this dismissive interpretation they uncovered powerful tradeoffs; that is, to produce the director's "mountain-girl" stories would have meant overriding the self-image the girls themselves valued. Or, using the failure frame's focus on what didn't happen ignored the digital skills the girls did choose to learn. Once again, metacognitive reflection supported by a sophisticated conceptual frame generated and transformed knowledge.

When Analysis Becomes a Working Theory

We left Josh trying out his new consultant's listening frame in one case and figuring out what to do with the competing frames he heard—once he actually listened to different readings of a college policy. Justine, heading back into high school teaching after finishing her master of arts degree in rhetoric, is concerned more directly with how her interpretations translate into action in teaching and, in her first case, to the tricky arena of family relations. Her metacognitive analysis starts by putting her chosen influential concepts to work:

> Rethinking the purpose of deliberation will make a substantial difference in my teaching. But on the personal side of things, West's notions of agency, prophetic pragmatism, and cultural critique were eye-opening for me . . . I know my uncle is homophobic. I know he comes from a generation in which homophobia was the norm, so I usually end up writing him

off as a fossilized bigot—mean-spirited and bitter, but basically harmless. I now see that my "basically harmless" judgment of him was an oversight on my part. Now, if my uncle were discursively isolated, a voice crying out in the wilderness, he could indeed be harmless. But as West says, we all—as individuals—are "inseparable from" the "moral and political judgments and the workings of a . . . critical consciousness" (24). Our culture shapes our opinions, true, but we in turn influence our culture. My uncle's opinion isn't just a mental fabrication that he keeps inside himself. That opinion is a vote. That opinion is a rude remark. That opinion manifests itself in ways that keep homophobia a part of our culture.

Choosing to resee herself in West's terms as a "culture worker" prompts a re-interpretation of a family encounter in the form of a model, albeit a small one, of an effort to "influence our culture":

Case in point: Three years ago, my family, including the above-mentioned uncle, was at my house on Christmas Eve [and something prompted] my uncle to launch into a story: "Oh yeah, I remember back in the 80s when those two faggots killed that kid—." Now, I didn't say anything to my uncle; the rule in my family is to avoid political discussions, which inevitably devolve into fights, at all costs. But I gave him a look—and soon realized that my three cousins (all in their early- to mid-20s) were also giving him the look. He must have noticed, as he cut himself off and tried to explain himself ("Well, that's what we called 'em back in the day," etc.) before fleeing to a different table with a homogenously older crowd.

To be sure, this is not some crowning moment in LGBTQ equality. It was well within my power to call my uncle out on the slur, even if I did end up "starting a fight," and I opted not to. But my cousins and I did send him a message that he heard loud and clear: "Use that language around us, and we won't talk to you." I say he heard it loud and clear because he hasn't used any homosexual slurs in my presence since then (although I'm sure he says plenty of them when I'm not around). The agency of the individual, and the notion of the individual as a cultural worker, have shifted my perception of what happened here. As I said, this moment does not mark some decisive victory in gay rights—but it does within my sphere. It is a victory that I helped create within the sphere in which I have power to make a change.

Moments of éclaircissement revealing our own casual assumptions—about that unquestioned silence dictated by family rules or the insignificance of one's own inaction—can be a step toward having a voice, initiating a family dialogue (or perhaps just becoming a family troublemaker). Moreover, Justine's story resonated with others in the class, just back from Thanksgiving break with families of Trump voters, prompting a group discussion of rhetorical options. These extended discussions of everyone's inquiry mark a critical next phase in this cycle. Articulating one's thinking gives everyone an enlarged understanding. But in this case, it also names the hidden frame, in the sense Freire and Heifetz share, as a problem that calls for dialogue. Given that Justine was not alone in dealing with that frame, this discussion phase created a shared space for exploring the subtle directions this "how-to" guide is giving and the ways it can play out in different life-worlds.

Be the Change You Want to See

I want to conclude with Justine's second case in point because it takes us into a final (visible) phase of her cycle of inquiry, where an articulated metacognitive analysis is being translated into a working theory. For Justine, the biggest impact on her personal and future professional life came from a challenge to her well-developed (and teacherly) interpretive frame for the nature of argument. But her new working theory goes well beyond a theory of argument:

> While I learned a lot about both leadership and dialogue this semester, I think the knowledge I've gained about the latter will have the biggest impact on my personal and professional lives. This class has profoundly altered the way I think of argument and deliberation, and these alterations will show in my teaching. Firstly, I now realize that, even as a student of rhetoric, I didn't even have a firm idea of what "argument" or "deliberation" meant before taking this class. I'd always assumed both more or less entailed a group of at least two people trying to sell one another on a position.

Notice how this soon turns into a richly embodied recollection that locates these rhetorical concepts in the world of a classroom (where she expects to find herself shortly) in an inquiry-squelching interaction with teachers and peers, ordered by a rule-governed tradition of teaching:

> I also realize that much of what I learned about argument and deliberation in high school (and about teaching argument and deliberation in high school) is, simply put, bad pedagogy. The most egregious example is the "debate." Several times throughout my high school career, I had to engage in class-wide debates

about contentious topics (the ones I remember most clearly were on abortion, the Indian Removal Acts, and the ethics of dog breeding). In all these debates, my teachers arbitrarily divided the class into two teams, one "pro-issue" and one "anti-issue." We then had a week or so to confer with our teammates and conduct research with the goal of defending our position at all costs. During the debates, our goal was to push for our side as much as possible while discrediting our opposition's arguments. At the end of the debate, we would usually vote anonymously to determine which side had "won."

This critical analysis of a traditional evaluative frame soon becomes transformed into a probing, well-articulated analysis of the implications this interpretive frame has for thinking. Translating educational meanings into actions, she articulates her own teacherly frames, which include how to teach argument, how to evaluate students, and the significance of students' own thinking:

This model of debate (which seems to fall under neither "argument" nor "deliberation"), I now realize, propagates many harmful beliefs and habits of mind. It assumes there are only two sides to any given issue, thus severely limiting the range of possible positions, options, and outcomes that may emerge in the debate. It assumes students' authentic beliefs about an issue don't matter. It assumes that pushing a position one doesn't truly support is not only acceptable, but positive. It assumes that "good argument" means cutthroat, uncritical defense of one's position. It assumes that other positions exist only to be negated. It assumes that the goal of debate is to prove to the "other team" that they're wrong. It assumes that changing one's mind during the course of the debate is a sign of weakness. It assumes that in any discussion, there are necessarily "winners" and "losers." And it assumes that persuasion is ultimately impossible: If the goal is to "win" (i.e., persuade the other side), but changing one's mind means losing, then who would admit to being persuaded? Needless to say, I will not be employing this deliberative strategy in my classroom . . .

In this detailed unpacking of an interpretative frame, we can see critical consciousness emerging in which a theoretical concept such as "deliberation" becomes a tool for a metacognitive analysis of her own frame for "teaching argument" (not to mention the problematic little package of ideological common sense being unpacked). Secondly, this level of analysis translates a problematic frame into the dynamics of thinking, evaluating, and interacting with students. In doing so, it lets her articulate actionable implications and alternatives—a working theory. Finally, it suggests the power of writing, prompted by conflict, to create actionable insight. As the paper ends, the working theory has begun to move into a statement of possibilities, a hypothesis about potential outcomes, and a sense of connection to an even larger educational controversy about difference. As Justine puts it:

> . . . and if the whole class is going to deliberate about a common topic, then it only makes sense that differences would have to be considered a resource. Were we to hold to the old assumption that differences are obstacles . . .

Chapter 5. Putting Transformation to Work

Always challenging our quest for certainty, John Dewey challenged the Greek attempt to locate the meaning of an idea, such as "knowledge," within a transcendent notion of Truth. Philosophical pragmatism would, instead, locate the meaning of a concept, such as "engaged education," in its consequences. What difference would it practically make to any one if this notion rather than that were true? In what respects would the world be different if this alternative or that were true? There can be no difference anywhere that doesn't make a difference elsewhere . . . (Quest 142).

A secondary principle of American Pragmatism would locate "understanding" (something our courses hope to engender) not in what is taught, or even is what is learned, but in action. Pragmatism could be characterized as the doctrine that all problems are at bottom problems of conduct, that all judgments are, implicitly, judgments of value, and that, as there can be ultimately no valid distinction of theoretical and practical, so there can be no final separation of questions of truth of any kind from questions of the justifiable ends of action (C. I. Lewis, qtd. in West, *Keeping Faith* 109).

The Case

This final case study was engendered by curiosity about just what some of the "notions" Dewey refers to could come to "mean." Students had described the Leadership, Dialogue, and Change course and engaging in its Think Tanks as a formative experience of some kind (see Chapter 2, Case 2). I wondered what the consequences, in terms of action, might look like four, six, eight or ten years later. This case study draws on a small, highly selective, but I believe revealing sample of the graduate students who had participated in one (out of four) of these classes over this ten-year period. One has to be skeptical about the quality and accuracy of recall over this amount of time. Memories are open to reconstruction and any "experimenter bias" of being interviewed by a former professor/friend. However, one indication of impact and the kind of knowing these discussions reveal comes through in the clarity and specificity of the outcomes they describe (as it does in critical incident interviews). Frequently articulated with energetic certainty, they are typically focused around two or three well-articulated memories developed with examples or stories, sometimes noting as one graduate put it: "I think about this a lot." What I think we can say about this method is that it captures best what stands out, after the fact, as strongly memorable to these students. And, I believe, it suggests how engaged humanistic courses can develop some widely valued forms of understanding and a body of working knowledge that is associated in these comments with self-conscious leadership, reflective decision making, and independent, self-initiated learning—capacities many disciplines are eager to claim.

The interview template was relatively open ended, in that it did not emphasize the recall of course material but each graduate's personal take away and use of the course or Think Tank experience. Sending my questions ahead, I essentially invited them into an inquiry with me that would pose four kinds of questions:

- Do you recall one or two of the most important ideas or insights you took away, not as content knowledge but as insights you may have constructed for yourself?
- Have you used what you learned or taught yourself in any place since?
- Did you need to adapt or even significantly transform what you learned to this new setting?
- And although this may be more difficult to articulate, did this experience transform your understanding in any way?

Although this analysis will draw most particularly on the lens of leadership and decision-making, three striking observations capture the overall character and tenor of these outcomes:

- First, they are highly variable—not a predictable reflection of what was being taught. They typically take the form of quite personal insights.
- Secondly, although the memory of a method or strategy frequently prompted recall, that recall quickly took the form of action that typically had public outcomes. Their learning had consequences for other people.
- And in the majority of cases, these outcomes reflected not simply a transfer of learning but a significant, purpose-driven transformation.

This evidence of transformation may in fact be the most important outcome revealed by this longer look-back. The chance to interpret powerful ideas and test theories against the challenges of community experience opened a path to transforming one's knowing, to creatively rewriting and adapting it to new situations and contexts. They are demonstrating one of the deeper values we can claim for education in the humanities. Especially when it is socially engaged.

Using the Lens of Adaptive Leadership

Leadership, tied to decision-making and teamwork, was a foundational concept in this course. It is a hot topic in research as well as in training programs emerging in writing, psychology, management, public policy. Its combination of theory and practice articulates a set of skills often developed in socially engaged education. So this lens can make a case that resonates outside our own discourse for the kind of transferable skill also valued by managers, educators, and social activists alike, needed in public, professional and community settings. It gives us a socially significant lens with which to evaluate the outcomes of learning.

It also gives us a solidly grounded template for looking at our data in terms of four significant outcomes. The first is evidence that students have been rethinking their own *definition* of leadership and its rhetorical nature. Unlike an action that is judged to succeed or fail, with this outcome students begin to re-represent leadership as a form of inquiry. Secondly, they speak to transformations in their own *self-image* as a leader who, quite unlike the expert in charge, is able (and willing) to realize the complexity of a problem and bring others in. A third outcome they described can be the emergence of a distinctive perspective that integrates *theory with the collaborative practices* (as we saw in the Think Tanks), which often leads to reflection on their current notions and a new working theory of what that change means. Finally, for some, their stances have matured into what they call their leadership *role* which, unlike a position of merely designated authority, has been learned. In our case, students will describe a practice that combines active listening with strategically framing an adaptive problem that will draw others into a joint problem-solving inquiry.

The source for this lens comes from Ronald Heifetz, whose work we read in the class (cf. Chapter 4). A noted scholar at Harvard's Kennedy School of Government, he nevertheless depicts an intensely rhetorical process he describes as "adaptive work" in *Leadership Without Easy Answers*. His conceptual lens will help us track a powerful outcome in which students have developed a new definition, self-image, stance and role that undergird the practice of adaptive, collaborative, inquiry-driven leadership. In traditional models the leader is a charismatic figure, an expert, or an authority, who frames the problem and by implication its solution. He (sic) draws others (the followers) into his vision. In Heifetz's model, however, leaders work as collaborative change agents, where success depends on being able to draw others to face what he calls "adaptive challenges." This stands in contrast to *technical problems* which "can be solved with knowledge and procedures in hand"—the standard ones for which you have ready-made answers. *Adaptive challenges,* on the other hand, often require "new learning, innovation, and new patterns of behavior" (Parks 10). Here success depends on something more difficult than marketing one's own vision, since the process can even call for "the transformation of long-standing habits and deeply held assumptions and values" just as we saw in Chapter 4.

Being a leader in such a situation calls for strategic work, not just a better argument or a charismatic personal style. The Think Tanks frequently plunged students into such challenges, in cross-hierarchy, intercultural rhetorical situations embedded in actual institutional decisions or concerns (such as creating a new Global Communication Center, recognizing a culture of stress on campus, or ways to deal with diversity). In this discussion, the term "strategic" refers to a kind of thinking that is planfully goal-directed, self-consciously adaptive, and open to change based on the test of experience. It stands in useful contrast to de Certeau's definition of "strategic" as an institutional power move and to the opportunistic, often practical "tactical" approach that Mathieu argues for (16).

Drawing instead on cognitive psychology, in the alternative approach used here "strategic" moves grow out of a more reflective process of choosing an action you can articulate and justify, then using that experience to develop and adapt that strategy based on what you learn.

Decision research can also help us identify other features of adaptive, collaborative leadership that engaged courses are good at developing. For instance, in the face of a decision a savvy leader will recognize the power of diversity and small group meetings over large gatherings. In fact, the "best approach may well be a series of interviews with individuals" because the "most important element is the *diversity* of perspectives you assemble" (Johnson 52). Why? Because this move lets you overcome the "unconscious response in humans to discuss elements that are commonly known to other members of the group,"—the groupthink that stifles innovation (52). A small group deliberation has a critical, individual cognitive dimension as well, because the "challenge, of course, is how to trick your mind into perceiving that third option, or the fourth or fifth lurking somewhere behind it" (52)—this is the "challenge of [what Johnson calls] full-spectrum thinking" (55).

Once again this is an educational issue. Early research by Paul Nutt argues forcefully for the need to *learn* such a skill. His first insight was the positive correlation "between the number of alternatives deliberated and success" (Nutt, qtd. in Johnson 67). Unfortunately, he also found that only twenty-nine percent of organizational decisions he studied considered more than one alternative. And teenagers barely edged them out with thirty percent when confronting personal choices. Moreover, there also appears to be a strong correlation between astute decision-making and recognizing—and embracing—uncertainty (56).

The Heifetz model, developed with powerful case studies drawn from dilemmas ranging from civil rights politics to environmental regulation to patient/doctor relationships, illustrates adaptive leadership in action. But does that imply that a college course can do more than describe this powerfully interactive kind of knowing? Motivated by the reputation of Heifetz's overflowing 90-seat classroom in Harvard's Center for Public Leadership, Sharon Parks fortunately undertook an intriguing, multi-year study of his approach, published as *Leadership Can Be Taught*, which will give us yet another lens for examining teaching outcomes more directly.

The educators' problem is reflected in the assumption that "leaders are born, not made." Can the academic paradigm of transferring knowledge actually "prepare people to exercise the judgment and skill needed to bring that knowledge in the intricate systems of relationships that constitute the dynamic world of practice" (Parks 4)? Moreover, "people must learn to *see* for themselves" and they "learn best from their own experience" (4–5). What Parks describes is a form of case-in-point teaching which includes some outcomes that could be used to document leadership learning in our own students. The most obvious outcome is being able to move from theory to practice as a participant. In

Heifetz's inventive terms, that is called moving from the balcony (where one can see larger patterns of interaction) to the dance floor. Once on the floor, students must be able to identify the primary concerns their specific group sees, as well as the "subtle, powerful, and unexamined assumptions they [themselves] hold" (51).

Developing leaders need to show they can think systematically about interdependent forces with "a critical, systemic, holistic perspective" (Parks 53). This includes recognizing/transforming some of one's own assumptions about leadership. The community-engaged course then works as a "holding place" to work on this transformation in which we realize we are not "in charge" or even autonomous in this radically interdependent world. Nevertheless, the actions we do take may have more effect than we supposed. We are all complicit. Finally, leaders need to regularly and persistently ask: "What are the (adaptive) challenges that are emerging" here, now (59)? Using a Heifetz lens brings into focus how a person's way of defining leadership, their own self-image, and role—from multiple perspectives—can add up to a distinctive practice of *adaptive, collaborative, inquiry-driven* leadership.

As we have seen, a community Thank Tank is a learning lab immersing student in deliberative leadership that starts with their exploration of a problematic issue using Critical Incident Interviews (Chapter 2, Case 2.). As we have seen, the competing perspectives they uncover and document in their Briefing Book give direction to a series of student-moderated Round Table discussions, in which a cross-section of the relevant "community" is asked to define the Problem, identify Options, and consider possible Outcomes. When the new, richly articulated foundation for deliberation and action is documented in the student-written *Findings*, it can be put into circulation as both a booklet and published on the web. Throughout the process, these students are engaged in a live experience with a generative problem-solving process where outcomes actually matter. This may explain why nearly everyone in this study talked about this process of inquiry as a key takeaway, even as they adapted it for some radically different contexts and goals.

In terms of tracking, we will approach the transcribed data from my interviews from three perspectives. First, we do so by focusing on what stood out as three topics of major concern for these students: an evolving definition of leadership; changes in their self-image; and the connection between theory and practice. A second approach lets us examine this data in terms of those markers of success that we saw in the leadership research. Finally, our analysis will probe three major categories of knowledge outcomes they raised (capacity for inquiry, collaboration, and strategic response) and how they frame the markers of success. Table 5.1 lets us compare these three modes of interpretation. Designed to highlight some of the parallels between them, it not only helps us elaborate different facets of this "knowing" as James Greeno and his colleagues described it (100), but see the wider significance and reach of these transformations.

Table 5.1. Parallels between Perspectives of Students, Research, and Observation

Key topics the graduates brought up were	Learning research sees growth when students can	Knowledge outcomes can be described as
A revised definition of leadership as a process of inquiry	Take a critical, systemic perspective on a consciously adaptive process	Articulated critical insights from an inquiry, yielding both metacognitive and working knowledge
A transformed self-image and role	See themselves as implicated in the process—not in charge	A working knowledge of collaboration across difference
A new perspective on theory and practice learned from experience	Can move from the balcony to the dance floor	Actions that combine rhetorically attuned understanding with a strategic response

What We Observed

The following analysis explores the nature of the knowledge outcomes from the right-hand column in Table 5.1, fleshing out the three distinctive kinds of knowing these graduates appear to have constructed and the uses they are putting them to. Briefly described they are:

1. **Articulated critical insights.** Engaged education replaces a spectator theory of knowledge-making with an experiential one—it places us in the arena, in action. It calls out what John Dewey described as "experimental doing for the sake of knowing." To understand the nature of an idea, "we turn it over, bring it into better light, rattle and shake it, thump, push and press it . . . disclosing relations that are not otherwise apparent" (*Quest* 70). Dewey's metaphors anticipate a process we might describe today as embodied learning with material effects. He wants to make this distinction perfectly clear: "inquiry proceeds by reflection, by thinking . . . but *not*, most decidedly as something cooped up within 'mind.' For experimental inquiry or thinking signifies *directed activity,* doing something which varies the conditions under which objects are observed and . . . by instituting new arrangements among them" (99).

In addition, the most powerful insights students describe are typically based on the *outcomes* of their own embodied experience—their encounters with difference, uncertainty, unexpected conflict, unanticipated success. As Dewey would argue, you grasp the real meaning of an idea when you can describe the "conditions" in which it can exist and its "consequences." "From the standpoint of experimental knowing . . . the true object of knowledge resides in the consequences of directed action" (157). And it is "the consequences" of actions and their "connectivity within concrete experience" that let us test the nature and validity of ideas (92). And finally, as we will see in students' accounts of this engaged learning, their inquiry has achieved an impressively articulated clarity. It is rising to this level of reflective metacognitive understanding that can turn learning into a basis for choice.

    2. **A working knowledge of collaboration across difference.** Rooted in experience and designed for performance, such metacognitive understanding also remains open to change, able to function as a working hypothesis. And in this case, the performance entailed collaboration across differences in race, culture and status.

    3. **A rhetorically attuned understanding and strategic response.** This may be one of the least documented yet most significant outcomes a liberal education aspires to. The experience of facing challenges in highly interactive, social or public contexts is transformed into a rhetorically attuned understanding that can guide a strategic response.

Articulated Critical Insight

This first outcome to which students often referred was a significant insight or challenge to previous thinking, and in some cases, it was a formative experience. Some insights were recalled as one of those sudden realizations, while others appeared to be larger in scope, more profound or personal. Martha's memory is explicit.[1]

> I have this moment, can still see it in my head, where I was sitting over in the cafe reading this and just having this like ah ha, whoa, this is like holy cow, just like a moment of clarity . . .
>
> [On the Think Tank] One of the most profound things for me . . . was a process of thinking through a problem . . . looking at events or feelings and trying to embody multiple perspectives. First time I really tried to do that and I saw it worked! . . . Learned about what had happened, about my role in what happened and also how I could have done it differently or in the future.
>
> [Moreover,] that was really foundational for me, to think through problems and see that I had agency; didn't have to passively accept what happened in that case and other possible cases. [In contrast] to how I grew up, . . . it gave me a strategy for seeing that I could, not maybe radically change things, at least could influence them. That was really foundational for

---

    1. In the quoted excerpts which follow, editorial comments have been interpolated in brackets for clarity, including the topic of discussion. The speakers vetted this chapter and chose their own names.

> me and then I adapted that assignment and used it in my freshman class.

We might read this last point as an instance of the transfer of an assignment (albeit to a significantly different context). But the more revealing outcome was her articulation of what was actually a set of *experiential* goals for learning that shaped the design of her own course:

> I think honestly, I wanted them to have an experience that was similar to mine. To do that process of thinking through what happened and have those moments of realization . . . I wanted them to do what I did [laughs], but also plumb the depths of self-advocacy.

When asked about "usefulness," her comments switch to an on-going reflective process on her own social agency:

> Significantly useful. It really shaped everything . . . For me individually it was my most foundational academic slash life experience. And that's why maybe I'm still [eight years later] figuring out why that's the case. I think it has to do with problem solving; I think it has to do with recognizing possibility . . . even when it's like . . .

Leaders need her insight into the value of recognizing possibility despite difficulty. The challenge is translating that into knowledge you can use. Insights are more likely to become genuine working knowledge when they are transformed into *articulated* insights. Developmental psychologists Carl Bereiter and Marlene Scardamalia can see this outcome in the psychological transition young (and poor) writers can make from "knowledge-telling" to "knowledge-transformation." In knowledge-telling writers can rehearse (or even knowledge-dump) what they already know. But "transformationrequires moving from a "content space" into a "rhetorical space" which demands rethinking, reworking one's knowledge into more responsive and fully developed thoughts. It is this "interaction between problem spaces . . . that is the basis for reflective thought in writing" ("From Conversation" 11). We can see Martha as a writer in the act of articulating and transforming old interpretive accounts of her potential:

> I never felt like I was doing something, like I was making something happen . . . [It] spoke to the difficulty of getting people to do things, or changing things for the better. It just made me see it was possible—but that it was also really difficult. And that is something that has probably stuck with me, since . . . I think it is something that shows up in my dissertation too, that it's possible, but it's hard. A lot of work. But for me that was hopeful because I think prior to that I think I thought it was like "What's the point?" You know these things could be changed,

and should be changed, but *I* [emphasis added] certainly don't have the resources or the wherewithal, or the ability or the whatever, the authority to change them. And I think I learned that it wasn't about me necessarily, and that I could, we could, it's just kind of a matter of embracing the uncertainty and seeing the possibility . . . Spoke to like hope.

Throughout these case studies of adults, we are seeing a remarkable degree of self-awareness linked to a style of metacognitive inquiry. They have made the experiential leap from Bereiter and Scardamalia's potentially "inert knowledge" into actionable understanding—a leap which is the mark of engaged education ("Knowledge"181). This self-awareness often includes a situated recognition of contradiction within their own experience, as seen by Megan below:

My take away? It challenged ideas about what I thought leadership meant . . . as something you either succeed or fail at. For example, I taught a lesson in class that didn't go the way I thought it was going to go so I identified that as failure of leadership. After talking with you and my peers, we realized that that wasn't the problem . . . it was how I approached the situation, didn't fit the context appropriately. So one of the things I learned is it's really about taking positions of inquiry in deliberation. That it's really all very contextually based. Which make a lot of sense. Silly I didn't think of that before because we study rhetoric [laughs].

For Devon, learning new tools of inquiry turned into what he called his "major revelation" when he felt the contact with the social reality of writing:

That was the eye-opening. Forced to think about own writing. It was a break through moment to think about: what is my purpose for writing? At that point I was, "I'm writing this paper for the teacher who likes . . ." [And then] I personally just said, "No I'm writing for myself. What am I trying to achieve? What are *my* purposes? What is my plan? I'm writing for the larger community and what do I want to do?"

When rhetorical and analytical methods (in this case, collaborative planning and problem analysis) are both studied and put to use in a context that can push back, students may learn as much about their own unquestioned practices as about the tools. In the cases which follow, students will often refer to a specific, research-based, named strategy that was used, discussed and adapted to the project at hand. (See Chapter 2, fn. 13 for an overview.) But what matters is what they *did* with it.

What stands out about this sort of outcome—these articulated insights—is how they have moved into so many different life situations, from writing and teaching to reflecting on your upbringing and the possibility of personal agency. Of course, this is what education is supposed to do. But note how these outcomes are couched in the multi-faceted language of experience shaped in social interaction. And like the sensitive quills of a porcupine, such knowledge can be easily triggered by all manner of new events. From the first Community Think Tank, this way of representing ideas had emerged as a distinctive outcome. Unlike a standard academic or policy deliberation, these "results" were being framed as actionable take-aways relevant to the participants and their differing social, cultural, and workplace domains. This, I would argue, is the added value of engaging with new ideas on the playing field of social experience.

A Working Knowledge of Collaboration across Difference

If the first set of comments captures the articulation of insight that experiential learning can prompt, another category of outcomes shows that new understanding being developed into what I have called *working knowledge* (Flower, "Intercultural Knowledge"). That is the sort of knowledge that may be theory-based or a hypothesis but in a form tied to practice—a kind of knowing that *works*. Here we see learning being put to active use in the individual's own research, teaching, and, well, in places you might not expect. In these accounts, one practice that frequently rises to the surface is the student's new understanding of collaboration and the role of conflict.

Teamwork, of course, is highly valued in many of the professions students are aspiring to and is frequently assigned rather than taught in many disciplines in college. Moreover, instructors are "rarely aware of the problems students are facing" (Wolfe v) and students often equate teamwork with merely the most efficient division of labor (Rooney et al.). By contrast, the working knowledge the Think Tank graduates describe seems much closer to the best practices from teamwork research, which can range from serious listening and eliciting silent stories to using difference and managing productive conflict (Paulus and Yang). And when that difference also includes race, gender, culture, and status, how many standard college courses are ready to equip students with more than good intentions?

Westin was facing his own challenge as a white man committed to working across racial difference in a community project. Speaking of the leadership course:

> This was my most sustained teamwork project I have ever done, still have ever done. I thought that was really great because you don't get that in the humanities . . . When I think about my ability to work on a team, I mostly think about this . . . In an ideal sense you are drawing out other people's strengths.

Megan had a more personal response.

> Writing together was really useful for me. It took some of the pressure off me, like feeling I had to craft perfect language ... It was 100% collaborative and it took some of the burden of perfection off me.

For some, their working knowledge shows up as a key practice in their own research, especially in this case from Maureen when that research is actually focused on professional teamwork:

> Most memorable, first is ... the critical incident interview. Being able to ... reveal some of the tacit knowledge, ... [which] they would not be able to reveal ... if you just asked. Versus summarize. Tacit knowledge is one thing I'm trying to tap into with professionals ... [Laughs] So I definitely think about [these two ideas] kinda all the time. Talk about transformation!
>
> Another thing is group work—also part of my dissertation [laughs]. When I think back to the most memorable collaborative experience that I've had, that class with the think tank was the most memorable group work that I've I had. There were challenges we faced, but the collaboration we did, part of my research is also on productive conflict. When I think of the ideal situation where I engaged in productive conflict, that project immediately pops into my mind. We'd get together, have our own viewpoints, then we would challenge each other, pull apart ideas ... then like merge things together. Yeah, it was incredible. I enjoyed every single minute of it. (Maureen)

As Craig Moreau discovered, this sort of productive conflict fostered by difference-driven inquiry was a real driver of innovation in professional teamwork ("Teams"). However, in the professional writing courses he then studied, student teams were marked by conflict avoidance and even found it "counterintuitive." Happily, his workshop on strategies for "productive conflict" produced some statistically significant changes. But dealing with conflict is not easy, as he concluded: "students need more scaffolding to see difference as a generative resource" ("Teaching" 29). Experience with situations in which your innovation might count is the ideal scaffold.

As teamwork research also notes, homogeneous groups do indeed build better social bonds but not necessarily better work (Woolley and Malone). And Maureen's experience with community inquiry locates her team's productive bonds in the value of a more widely shared engagement across difference.

> Homogenous? There was definitely diversity. [She reviews the team's makeup: two MAs, three undergrads, Hispanic, non-native speaker, first generation, and privileged backgrounds.]

> We talked about outside experience and pulled on those to help us come up with different plans like . . . how do we get the administration involved [She describes how one member pulled on his experience on the student paper, "like these are some things we do" and another on "connecting to roots" in non-profit outreach.] We just pulled on these different things. It's like I have no experience doing either of those things. That's amazing. What can WE do to help out.

Although the critical incident interview is basically a research method, her representation of it sounds much more like a stance to research that became tested and refined.

> I initially went into the critical incident interviews with the understanding that you're constantly trying to push people to be a little bit more accountable to the things that they say and to explain those things in more detail . . . [However, the working knowledge she went on to develop is more clearly about the interactive nature of inquiry.] But I also remember [in yet another piece of research] I kept on trying to push them too far because I was looking for something that wasn't there, so I realized I need to be a little more perceptive about when to stop. (Maureen)

In particular, roadblocks and problems that challenge assumptions often produce such realizations. This graduate continued:

> Another thing I really took away was how to bridge gaps between different stakeholders. When we talked to admin, students, faculty, I remember the big thing was [whether] there was communication or lack of communication and misconceptions about what other groups thought . . . I remember [at a round table, some of the administrators] had absolutely no idea what was going on with the students, just like so mind blowing to me; how do you guys not know this? It's right in front of your faces, right under your nose! Then I realized there is a certain kind of information that just gets circulated in these groups. And because there can be such insularity . . . that it's really hard to be aware . . . Yeah, of course, people should be talking to one another, but taking that class made me really realize the gravity, the importance of getting people to communicate with one another across these differences. Now it's something even in my research I am trying to bridge, in technical communication [in college and workplaces]. (Maureen)

Difference takes many forms. In this next excerpt Andre describes a technique he, as a teacher, imported into his Public Problems course. (His students called the technique "a kind of Creative Thinking.") When I asked if there were any parallels to our course, his response was rather emphatic.

> Useful? Oh yeah, oh my gosh, absolutely. The process of Rivaling. For writing proposals . . . Shaped how I taught. Constantly trying to get students to think about alternative perspectives or how adequately are they representing the voices of other people who have a stake in this issue. (Andre)

Here a strategy for responding to difference could mean a fundamental shift is how you envision stakeholders and an audience. It's not like

> who you are writing to in academic lit or to people you are writing about in your topic area, but they are the people who live right next door to you or [whom you] attend classes with that are making decisions . . . Having had some experience dealing with a public problem in the Think Tank, where the stakes are real, . . . absolutely influenced [my teaching].

Of course, it's reassuring to see the usefulness of specific applications you may teach toward (as when students say, "I did value being able to bridge theory and practice.") Or when a graduate comments: "I think back to think tank approaches and how I can implement them in my research right now" or with a graduate advisor. However, other uses—of say, problem analysis—turn up in unlikely places:

> Another big takeaway—naming things, giving something a name. . . . in my research and in my personal life . . . being able to have a reference that links a bunch of ideas together and being able to talk about it . . . My boyfriend and I get into debates . . . Politics, . . . we unpacked this term conservative . . . where it came from . . . I was telling him, there just wasn't a term conservative, (it) described values . . . (Maureen)

What these comments help document is first how the knowledge people describe is not just propositional, but is a form of working knowledge. That is, that special form of knowing that is grounded in concepts, theory, or methods, but has also been transformed into socially embedded practices (like persuading your boyfriend). And the well-articulated character of this conceptual understanding is what makes those practices both testable and revisable. This second outcome, not surprising for a community-based experience, is the enthusiastic capacity we see for working collaboratively across difference. This striking outcome can be hard to come by in academic settings (Bennett et al.).

A Rhetorically Attuned Understanding and Strategic Response

Perhaps the most intriguing and complex outcome of engagement is this third one: the sophisticated form of knowing that emerges when students *try out* both theory and rhetorical practice *in live contexts*. The experience not only prompts them to draw on learned insights, but to do so with a more rhetorically attuned understanding of the situation. They are able to transform knowing into thoughtful and strategic responses to challenging social interactions. Secondly, they are doing this with a remarkable level of metaknowledge that lets them articulate and evaluate their own choices. From an educational point of view, as we saw in Ryan Roderick's work on self-regulation (Ch 2) documenting this level of reflective and clearly conceptualized self-knowledge can make a powerful statement about learning and the usefulness of engagement.

Having evidence of longer-term effects is obviously relevant to our case for the humanities and engaged education in particular. Can we show that such courses build not only personal agency and social responsibility, but also skills valued in our public and professional lives? How do these skills stack up against social expectations for, say, productivity, knowledge building, teamwork, or leadership? The interview questions asked these graduates for evidence of transfer, such as, if or when they used the course or the Think Tanks tools for inquiry on their own. However, the following accounts are better described as the result of a *transformation*.

In this process of adaptive re-creation, the first step is often not tinkering with a rhetorical tool but working from a new starting point they described as a change in "how I think about . . ." Or "how I approach . . ." And from here graduates describe the experience of strategic knowledge building, creating related but novel moves, intentionally adapted to specific challenges, from leadership to job hunting.

In a nice example of traditional transfer, a graduate laughingly describes how, yes, the various methods of the Think Tank shaped her own research: "I used the Think Tank method to motivate my dissertation research method . . . How to bring people together to collaboratively solve a problem." But when asked if she has thought any more broadly about the model of leadership we studied, her picture of on-going, creative, self-directed performance emerges:

> I never stopped thinking about it. Taught it to my first-year writing students, then [a colleague] and I organized a conference [for a national organization] on how to be a graduate leader . . . I think of my research as being about writing as leadership. . . being an academic leader . . . I think about that a lot . . . ["About" I ask, "transforming your understanding?"] Transformed the way I think about leadership . . . Informed the way I see myself as a leader . . . When you first gave us that assignment, I thought, "I don't see myself as a leader." Transformed the way I think about

> my work, ... now as a professor ... as a woman ... and having a role in the university where I have some power. (Amy)

> I don't think it was like "transfer." For me it was more individual, it kind of influenced how I approached what I was doing, whether it be teaching, my own research, my own [laugh] life. I think it helped me keep asking questions. ["How come?" I ask.] Because I embraced the idea that problems are never as simple as we think they are ... Bringing in other people. That has really stuck with me on so many areas ... But I feel like that problem-solving stance has to be adapted. (Martha)

For Dasen, the process of "adapting" starts with a new way of thinking about problems and collaborative leadership from which he creates some original, inventive practices of his own.

> The Think Tank process was very illuminating ... What I learned from that, what I took away as valuable from that, "We think we know ... Oh, here's a problem; here's the solution." We think we know the solution. Well, we really don't know the solution. We've got to get behind the solution; we've got to investigate. And I've taken that in two different ways.

Which for him turns out to be not just two, but a set of radically different adaptations to being an executive officer in an organization, on the one hand, and to being a part-time student, on the other.

> And when I first took over [this leadership position] I actually sat down and talked it out with each of department heads to find out what are the issues, what am I not seeing, and how can I best assist. These questions, these techniques are things I think I learned from the Think Tank. And I also learned ...

As he goes on to describe these situated, reflective translations, their strategic, adaptive nature becomes clear.

> On the job market ... I invoked my experiences with the community think tank, I even gave ... them a copy of the ... materials and ... link to the website, that I was a part of! ... To demonstrate I've got some experience thinking about these larger issues ... Got offered a job. So it helped [laughs]. ... I'm thinking about rhetoric and leadership from both a theoretical and practical perspective—and in my dissertation as well. [And that was not all.] And I've applied it in different situations, in my home life: just talking to people and listening to people and really getting the Story-Behind-the-Story.

There is clearly an impressive individual personal stance that stands behind this portrait of knowledge transformation across contexts. It builds on a disposition and ability that is not *created* by a class, however strong its reported impact. On the other hand, from the perspective of leadership and decision making, one outcome more directly attributable to engaged learning is this strategically constructed metaknowledge which gets articulated as his "own leadership style." The capacity for such knowledge making clearly has reach, showing up in both teaching and in the following case, in job hunting.

> I thought about it as a listening tour. I actually use the phrase, "a listening tour." That's what I got out of me doing interviews for our Think Tank. Essentially what I am doing is listening. That's part of my leadership style . . . listening to people I may necessarily have authority over . . . people who are involved may have better ideas, better strategies. (Dasen)

In teaching returning veterans, he, like Martha, adapts collaborative planning to recreate his own learning experience, to get them, as he says, "at the beginning, to help get them thinking, to stimulate metacognition."

Another feature of socially engaged learning is the way it can disrupt not just prior knowledge, but practice. As Megan relates, the community context "challenged some ideas I had about what leadership meant and how I see myself in relation to that concept." What Megan recalled, however, is not just a tool or method but how this experience with a demanding situation shaped her performance, as well as her attitude and confidence.

> Having to the facilitate a Round Table itself . . . [in a later] similar situation I felt a little more comfortable jumping in . . . asking "could you go back to . . .?" Felt I would be able to adapt, to react to what others might do or say.

This comfort dealing with problem-solving, inquiry and/or uncertainty also turns up in changes in her practice in teaching and research.

> [Another] thing I think about a lot, that's rivaling . . . That's something I find myself doing with myself with the work I do . . . Analyzing something and I think "This is what the problem is or I am reading it this way?" I say well, what if it's not that way, what if it's something else, or why do you think it has to be that way, why can't it be something else?
>
> [In teaching] It make me feel less prescriptive . . . Now a little more flexibility in what you can do in a classroom. Now, "here's the goal, if it doesn't happen that way, we'll figure it out!"

Because the experience of a community-engaged class working toward real outcomes can raise the stakes and relevance of one's choices, it is more likely to force a reconsideration of old assumptions.

> Working with people I would never otherwise work with, exposed me to different ideas and different approaches to tasks, and I remember thinking, "Why did they do it that way! I didn't do it that way!" . . . Initially it was uncomfortable; I didn't like it, cause I couldn't control it [laughs], but . . . now I can see the connection to . . . working with different faculty members . . . to see things from their perspective. (Megan)

The challenge of carrying out effective social interactions comes up frequently in these comments. For Andre like Dasen it starts with reading the situation. For him what "stuck" as the "Number 1 insight from the readings" was the "ways people conceptualize problems in a deliberative or decision-making space . . . It shaped the way I think about problem[-solving] strategies . . ." More significant was the next step when he used Heifetz's distinction between technical and adaptive problems to shape a strategically attuned understanding of what was happening in a non-profit organization he had started to work with.

> In the midst of a discussion, in the back of my mind I recognized, as I was hearing what the person was saying. [It was that] tendency to gravitate to, "Oh let's find a solution" . . . [in place of] a more labor-intensive process of figuring out what their problem looks like from multiple perspectives, then actually figuring out a way forward that weighs those against each other . . .

This sort of "fundamentally useful" metaknowledge, which he attributes to "doing the interviews for that course work," in turn shapes his strategic response. In practical situations and his own research, you need to know:

> How to think on your feet about the kinds of questions you are asking and what you want to get from that interview. How to reflexively handle myself in these situations. (Andre)

The path of transformation, however, is not straight forward. Some, like this graduate student Westin, explicitly reject or "don't relate to transfer," focusing instead on the work of building their own model which Westin describes as: "I watch you, saying, 'I am going to also take a stand in this difficult thing.' You gave me one model or template for doing that." The path Westin recalls involves both difficulties and potential outcomes, starting with his skepticism about the whole practice of local deliberation, and his question:

> Is that [process] successful when it becomes institutional? . . . Not sure . . . At the time I was much more skeptical.

Yet in the next breath:

> This was the most productive entry point for me in all of my course work about thinking through an individual scholar's agency within an institution. By far. Who else even tries?

Speaking on the "model" he saw:

> It was a very difficult class to know what we were learning at the moment. But I think that's your teaching philosophy, so . . . I continue to think about Heifetz's "technical" versus "adaptive challenge."

As an aside, he notes:

> I thought in a faculty [job] interview, how I would be able to politely ask, "What's the last adaptive challenge that your department has faced?" And if they can't say anything, that would be a sign to me. [laughter]

Then back to the difficulty of all the new terms,

> But what I eventually internalized is, I name them as scaffolding strategies for getting people to talk. I've really taken that question with me.

When I ask: "The question?" he replies:

> How do we scaffold people into inquiry?

Not a small question. As Westin suggests, this path of transformation is often motivated not by the current situation, but by the desire to nurture an aspiration or vision in a complex (sometimes seemingly intractable) social setting or institutional practice.

Our final account of transformation introduces just this sort of dilemma, suggesting why learning in the context of a live, socially engaged learning experience may be so significant when we pose the question: So what?

> The biggest impact was the power of how you define a community problem . . . [As in, "We don't have an XXX Center."] We were assuming we had the solution in how we were defining it. A big moment for me . . . the process of redefining . . . Number One I think. That continued to stay with me as I became involved in university work . . . I became very attuned to how people were defining the problem at hand . . . Transformed for me how to participate . . . and how to take on leadership roles [when you need to] get people to define a problem in a different

way. Doing that in a meeting was something I think I got from doing the Think Tank. (Katherine)

The capacity to draw folks into re-defining a problem was called into play again when Katherine's campus group had, as she said, already dived into the "rabbit hole of getting data" on the solution to a problem they had already framed as "We need a Child Care Center!" To replace that process of solving a "technical" problem with inquiry, Katherine reframed the proposed solution as a question: "Well what were the issues the graduate students were having . . .?" And her approach was to pose that question at a regional conference, where the tendency was,

> they always want to make a survey. My take was . . . we started hosting lunches on their experiences . . . mixed with critical incident interviews . . . [And] found out we needed to understand what people were already doing . . . [and recognize there had been a] big change in graduate demographics.

The strategic nature of her knowledge transformation (into what she calls "certain principles I followed") stands out when the members of the national project she directed wanted to devise a strategic plan. In making their case, many groups wanted

> to produce a student bill of rights. . . . In a leadership role it felt to me like a big choice that really weighed on me. On the one side, there was the more activist side. Framing [the response] as a bill of rights had the potential to empower students. On the other hand, what the community think tank bought into the picture was "What does it mean when you're trying to make an institutional change?" . . . I remember you saying, "But how do you think [that an administrator] is going to feel when she reads, or . . . the department head . . . you are going to circulate this around campus . . ." It kind of became my approach to dealing with the graduate students. It opened me up to having to think about other institutional actors and also hierarchy . . . Doing the community think tank helped me think strategically about how to use certain forms of hierarchy, bringing certain people into these things, and how you often needed their leverage.

Her comment about a simple exchange between student and professor is a nice example of constructing a practice from an idea. Like a Bakhtinian utterance that implies a response, Katherine translates my simple problem-posing question into a model of intervention and interaction. And that transformation occurred, as is often the case, when a conflict pops up, well after the class is over.

> There were things I didn't get at the time. Like trying to make the Think Tank reporting be "dialogic." Don't think I really quite got that [laughs.] . . . Maybe I understood the principle of it, but it wasn't until I was in a situation where I could start the see the problems [when the group] wanted to create institutional policy like documents, wherein they had a very clear solution of what they were trying to go for and I'd walk into the meeting, knowing "No one's ever going to go for this." It's like one idea; it's not budging; it's not showing other perspectives; we're doomed . . .
>
> I began to see, "oh right, when we go into these things, we need to bring in, we need show a bit of a dialogue." Somewhat similar to what they talk about as transfer, but I don't think it was something I got and I was transferring; it was more like a delayed, putting-it-together. I felt like it was always at times when it felt like something didn't work.
>
> At the time I thought that part of trying to represent this in a dialogic way came out of a sense of principle that that was somehow also the right thing to do, to represent all the different stakeholders, but I think it was in these moments of also seeing it as a strategic move.

Katherine's description of "using things from this class" extends to a controversial choice between working like an

> activist ("We just need to go on strike!") or more like corporate leadership. . . . But how are grad students supposed to adapt to either of these models? So I was trying to find a way to use the approach in the community think tank model. It had a way I could see it straddling or blending parts of this . . . It spoke to a position graduate-student leaders are often facing . . . Which model, what kind of framework am I using to approach this?

For this graduate, the process moves into a larger intellectual arena of shaping educational policy and the experience of negotiating among different problem frames. But the cognitive move is not the transfer of tools, but rather a way of constructing a challenging new question for herself as an act of inquiry. Note, too, how this form of knowing is built progressively, a constructive process set in motion when she encounters a new problem. Along this path, her "biggest insights" come to influence

> my own research interest in education policy . . . This class actually started to shape my research interest, trying to understand, if the problem I was really interested in was how to change or how to shape some these policies. A lot of the focus was always

> on these critiques ... and the thing that was the big shift for me after this class and for my later work, was actually looking to, "Well, what were other people either in higher education or in other professional organizations, what were they doing that influenced, or didn't, any of this other stuff?" I think there was an orientation shift ...

When this focus on inquiry turns up in teaching, it is again on a personally defined problem

> I can't teach a community literacy course ... A dream course. So I adapt. [In her workshop on writing a research proposal, she sees the educational goal as seeking] knowledge that we don't have, something that we need to understand ... [on the] problem, defining and how we make that compelling.

As other participants have mentioned, the desired outcome of this teaching goes well beyond transfer to instead construct the kind of experience she had had.

> wanted them to see with their own experience, as students, their own senses of expertise ... Create something where they had some level of their own situated expertise to bring to it ... build from community problems here. (Katherine)

Like her aspiration to create dialogic encounters, this is a rhetorically strategic response emerging from both that "sense of principle ... the right thing to do" and sustained adaptive reflection.

It is rather hard to sum up all these innovations, interpretations, aspirations people see as linked to an often-distant experience in a course. That is as it should be, because what they are tracing are paths of transformation. Out of the interaction between theory and practice that engaged learning can offer, each has developed and can articulate a richer rhetorical understanding of new situations tied to their own distinctive, thoughtfully strategic response. Other community linked courses will combine academic ideas with personal engagement in different ways and are likely to produce different, but related learning outcomes. However, what we are seeing is the nature of learning that an engaged education is in fact creating–and the value of tracking it.

Chapter 6. Teaching for Transformation

Writing educators must challenge the public perception of writing, so argued Linda Adler-Kassner in her 2017 Conference on College Composition and Communication (CCCC) chair's address ("Because Writing"). As we noted in Chapter 1, she targeted the impoverished perception of what writing does as a force that shapes not only communication but also learning, identity, ideology, ideas and change. But she saved her well-documented attack for the economically motivated re-definition of instruction as a fast and narrow chute to a job which contributes to the economy. This route to "the profitable moment" (326) has no place for embodiment or encounters with uncertainty, conflict, or contradiction, what she calls "troublesomeness." This reductive view has in turn spawned a tidy set of criteria which identify and calculate achievement with a measurable set of competencies designed for workplace success (322).

Like the "crisis in the humanities," this battle is being fought in operational terms over how we define and measure learning. When the very term *measure* replaces the goal of showing *evidence* of learning, we have reduced its more complex, ultimately more essential, outcomes to what is easy or convenient to count.

So one motivation for this research has been to explore ways to discover, document, and more publicly represent some of the significant and distinctive outcomes of community-engaged education. And on that foundation to advocate for the privilege of teaching at the intersection of rhetorical theory, research, and social experience that supports a fully engaged education. Yet as Adler-Kassner suggested, the problem is that we haven't effectively challenged the mindset and methods of *measurement* with an alternative art of documenting and publicly representing critical outcomes that reach beyond the classroom.

Working in that direction, one of the success stories of the past decade has been discovering ways to rethink the meaning of and ways to teach for transfer. At the same time, as we saw in Chapter 1, transfer is a very contextually attuned practice. And being aware of that is critical to effective teaching (Roderick). Teaching, that would support not only transfer but the *transformation* of knowledge, sets the stakes even higher. Upon encountering a new rhetorical situation, writers need to realize that their prior knowledge will need to adapt to a social interaction, that learned practices are subject to revision, and that the writer's identity is on view. Moreover, as educators we know there is no "best" way to do that—to prepare students to enter a social/cognitive/affective event in which, as Dana Cloud would say, "reality bites." Given the polymorphous nature of engaged education, I expect each of us has worked toward some version of these goals in our own circumstances.

I want to be clear that the case studies sketched in this book are not an argument for a particular curriculum. However, I do believe, that in combination the approaches explored here, point to two conceptual frameworks that can support more fully engaged learning. They do this work by posing useful questions we can ask of a course or project. One framework building on activity theory would ask: *how are we helping students engage with their project's larger activity system* by asking:

- First, are we reading a situation to uncover its Contradictions (where practices, ideas or values come in conflict in order to discover in them openings for Change?
- Then, how are we Collaborating within a Contact Zone across different perspectives, experiences, values? Are we partners in Inquiry or is difference an obstacle to be overcome?

A second framework would ask: how can we help students work as grounded-theory builders by asking ourselves:

- How might I adapt the process of Grounded-Theory Building to students' learning?
- Researchers use the powerful moves of Grounded-Theory Building to develop a normative theory. But can students use these moves to build a more contingent and adaptable Working Theory?
- And am I teaching Theory Building directly? Are my students translating theory into action guided by a new Metacognitive Awareness of their choices, decisions, and outcomes?
- Finally, the path to transformed and transformative learning will lie not in what we teach, but in what students do. The Grounded-Theory Guide which concludes this chapter invites students themselves to reflect on their own theory-informed process of engagement, and to articulate where have they had the most success and where the hurdles lie.

Engaging with a Larger Activity System.

Students in an engaged course may quickly realize they are entering some sort of educational adventure, but they may not recognize the complexity of reading and writing that is at stake in this new social/cultural/historical activity system, such as Yrjö Engeström describes ("Developmental Studies"). The course itself is an activity system: 1) working within the traditions of education, the university, the program, as well as the local norms of a community culture; 2) using mediating tools, including lectures, papers, grades, discussions, joint planning sessions, written guides and even local dialects; 3) operating with divisions of labor among students, teachers, TAs, program chairs, advisors, community organization staff and participants, each with their own role and place in the division of labor, hierarchy, and power structure. Among all those active forces they need to consider which ones are making a difference. And finally, how do students represent *themselves,* as well as the unvoiced contradictions, all within the larger activity system that their socially engaged class has entered? How does our course turn activity theory into a new way of seeing?

The practice of "early uptake" (see Chapter 3, Case 1) is a clear example of re-seeing which worked to understand the needs of Phoenix's South Sudanese immigrant women—before automatically sending them to one of the community's standard "literacy" classes (Long, *Responsive*). That means, before opting for a ready-made solution to what leadership theorist Ronald Heifetz calls a "technical problem," we are choosing to face a more demanding "adaptive" one. Recognizing the failure of many programs to be genuinely useful, this practice of "early uptake" started with listening and participating in order to understand the highly gendered economic and social power structures of the Sudanese diaspora community. Coming to grips with this complex and unfamiliar activity system uncovered some of its critical contradictions, such as an immigrant culture in which women have to be both primary breadwinners *as well as* family/home managers. This early uptake saw the striking incongruity between the genre-based assignments of the university's literacy outreach classes and the women's real uses for literacy as both personal sensemaking and advocacy. For educators to self-consciously grasp, much less play a role in, this activity system called for new tools, such as active observation or engaging in multi-voiced collaborative planning. As described by Elenore Long, Jennifer Clifton, and their associate Roda Nyapuot Kuek, this led to inventing a "positional mapping" practice that traced the "cultural flows" in this South Sudanese community, which, in effect, determined the expectations placed on these women (Long, *Responsive* 185–216). Working with this larger picture, their "responsive rhetorical art" had reverberations throughout its wider activity system.

A school-sponsored representation of a service or a course such as this is often built around what we are already prepared to do—what Heifetz would call managing that "technical problem" (8). To think beyond requires not only dipping your toes in an experience but thoughtful critical analysis, guided by powerful conceptual frameworks, such as activity theory or frame analysis. It is this ability to step back from the context provided in a college course and use its strategies to construct an equally complex but different representation of engagement—a transformation that occurs at the level of a social, cognitive, cultural and historical activity system itself.

Reading a Rhetorical Situation: Analyzing an Activity

A good place to engage this way of seeing is to analyze with your students the *rhetorical situation* they are entering—which is likely to be a particularly dynamic one. In the famous Bitzer/Vatz debate over this concept, Lloyd Bitzer's rhetor needs first to grasp the exigence, "an imperfection marked by urgency" (qtd. in Vatz 156). That is, to ask what stands behind this need to speak or write, right now (especially when it is not a mere assignment), which is linked to the nature of the audience and the constraints surrounding this situation? Richard Vatz's rhetor, however, also needs to recognize that the situation is created by what we choose to pay attention to and the interpretative act that translates it into meaning (157).

In "Political Rhetoric" Bitzer speaks even more directly to what the student must deal with, given some sort of evolving exigence an engaged course is likely to enter. Rhetorical concerns, then, are mainly probable, contingent, interest-laden, and frequently in contention. These characteristics mark the central realm of activity for rhetoric, which is the practical world of human affairs. Here rhetoric labors between the challenge and the fitting response, the imperfection and the remedy, the crisis and the calm. This, Kenneth Burke colorfully remarked, "is the area of the human barnyard—the big scramble" (qtd. in Bitzer, "Political Rhetoric" 8).

Has my class led students beyond acquiring a useful transferable genre, such as proposal writing or a public statement, into practicing the transformative art of probing, analyzing, interpreting, responding to the real rhetorical situation? (And are they also realizing that "real" is only a heuristic, an interpretive fiction we create in order to act?) Do they see their response to this situation as a step in Dewey's "experimental" way of knowing (*Quest* 132)? Not satisfied with comfortable or easy answers, our "knowing" is simply a current best hypothesis subject to the test of reality. This last point is perhaps essential to a meaningfully transformed application of learning: my classes and their expectations are over in 14 weeks—socially engaged situations tend to call for re-reading and reentering the fray.[1]

Conventional or narrowed readings of the rhetorical situation have consequences. David Coogan's well-supported argument for a materialist rhetoric described a dramatic, revealing failure when his class plunged into a campaign for neglected local public schools, publicly naming the problem as the need for "local control" (672). They read the situation as a familiar political advocacy call for neighborhood representation on local school boards. Unfortunately, they failed to uncover the politics of "local control" or share the residents' history with that agenda, which had merely resulted in surface policy changes soon co-opted by Chicago's city council.

---

1. In an intriguing case in point, Dr. Wayne Peck, director of Pittsburgh's Community House, trained two groups of community literacy interns to write an argument to the City Council advocating for a caring response to hunger in the inner city. One practiced the text-based strategies of Toulmin's data-warrant-claim scheme for argument. The other focused on a rhetorical representation of the participants and their goals—assessing values, attitudes, and beliefs and learning to strategically address the rhetorical complexity and social dynamics of the situation. Independent judges found that although the text-based instruction produced the best organized letters, they also agreed that they were unlikely to have any effect on the city council. It took the rhetorical/social instruction to create persuasive and powerful advocacy.

His class had entered a larger system that included a history and a set of rhetorical tools wielded by powerful institutions—such as the trick of assigning public titles and meaningless roles to citizens within an institutional structure. But in a subsequent—successful—attempt at community organizing for schools, Coogan drew on the more powerful tool of ideographic analysis, shifting his focus from political legislation to calling parents, students, and teachers to take "local responsibility" on themselves. Opening their eyes to the larger activity system and its contradictions led to redefining the problem, revising their rhetoric, and in some meaningful ways, rewriting the situation. It also worked.

Frame analysis is another powerful tool, especially when two frames are competing for turf in our activity. For instance, you may think of hunger with the standard "individualist" frame that tends to guide policy and the action of many non-profit "food-recovery" groups, where volunteers transport grocery stores' outdated surplus to local food banks. However, when Alex Helberg compared just this sort of non-profit, Pittsburgh's 412 Food Rescue, with another anti-hunger organization, he found them to be "vying for political hegemony" within the city, working from what he described as two radically different, competing "political imaginaries." (See also Chapter 4) Food Not Bombs, a local member of the anarchist movement, is a direct-action activist group. Its public potlucks are designed not only to raise awareness of and combat local hunger and food insecurity, but also to double as attention-getting political demonstrations.

412 Food Rescue's framework was designed to solve the "emergency" problem of hunger with methods of "food recovery," whereas Food Not Bombs attacks the individualist framing that dominates the broader political rhetoric. Hunger, they assert, is a large-scale societal problem (Helberg 7–8). The hungry people in Pittsburgh are evidence not of an *individualist* problem but a large-scale, societal, *systemic* problem.

So what can follow from an activity analysis of complex situations like these? As educators, we are good at giving students tools for different kinds of analysis (cultural, discourse, feminist, etc.), for making critical appraisals of rhetorical situations, and for constructing well-formed arguments in appropriate genres. Good analysis, however, is only a precursor to action.[2] In the case of community

---

2. In a challenging comparison of a high-stake formal education versus on-the-ground engaged learning, consider the forms of "non-traditional education" that go on in urban neighborhoods in crisis—in churches, Black newspapers, and community groups. This sort of engaged education comes to life when Derek Handley takes us into the historical and rhetorical resistance of three Black urban communities (Pittsburgh, St Paul, and Milwaukee) facing destructive "urban renewal" in the 1950s and 60s. His study shows us what a rhetorical education for community action had to accomplish. The leadership seminars in Milwaukee that sprang up had no small task: "to (develop) in students a communal and civic identity and [a program that] articulates the rhetorical strategies, language practices, and bodily and social behaviors that make possible their participation in communal and civic affairs" (Enoch 8–9, qtd. in Handley 106).

engagement, one of the real challenges is becoming collaborative partners across difference—and to not only overcome but to, in fact, put that difference to use (Flower, "Difference-Driven Inquiry").

Collaboration in a Contact Zone: Entering an Activity

As an engaged educator, the next question I would ask myself here is, how am I helping my student go beyond the *experience* of difference, as powerful as that may be, to interacting with self-awareness within a *contact zone*? An influential article by Louise Pratt back in 1991 defined contact zones as "spaces where cultures meet, clash, and grapple with each other, often in contexts of highly asymmetrical relations of power, such as colonialism, slavery or their aftermaths as they are lived out in the world today" (qtd. in Harris 31). However, as Joseph Harris argues, when Pratt's idea moves to the classroom, "many students have chosen to view the contact zone as a kind multicultural bazaar [defined by the voices on its reading list] which are not so much brought into conflict with opposing views as placed in a kind of harmless connection with a series of exotic others" (33). On the other hand, as Harris notes, faculty meetings also engage in the "wrangle of competing interests and views," and their model of interaction is equally problematic as "exchanges quickly devolved into a kind of position-taking, as the competing factions on both sides of the issue soon retreated back to and defended the very arguments they had entered the debate with" (35).

Though remaining rather understandably silent on the reform of faculty meetings, the alternative classroom Harris proposes is a contact zone in which students "negotiate the gaps and conflicts between several competing discourses" (31). He builds a case for just such "negotiation" that asks students to articulate and work through the differences they perceive among themselves as they discuss books or events (32). When, however, engaged courses move out of the designer space of a classroom, that zone is even less likely to be limited to general issues raised by race, gender, and status, or multicultural social theory. As Long's activity analysis showed, outside of the classroom students will be acting within the broader space of a rhetorical situation set in a social, institutional, and community setting.

The question then becomes, what happens when those students walk into a collaborative contact zone within the wider activity of engaged education? What

---

These seminars offer an exceptional model for engaged education within a community. In practice, Handley documents, they "empower(d) citizens with the knowledge of how the local government worked and the rhetorical skills necessary for leadership in their community. . . . creat(ing) the conditions for distributed agency in the fight against urban renewal and restricted housing. . . . By providing a safe space for residents to take control over their own circumstances. . . . [they] also helped residents establish relationships with other organizations and individuals outside the community" (117). The obvious question follows: how do our courses stack up?

if, as we saw in Chapter 3, their activity analysis must be attuned to a larger institutional system like a university, or their rhetorical analysis may have to deal with the current relationship between community members and their organizations? What if that "attunement" calls for drawing campus organizations, one's own professors, and college administrators into a new, deliberative public? And given that institution's norms, expectations, or rules for promotion, what does an activity analysis mean for an instructor—an untenured assistant professor teaching a 4/4 who chooses the special demands and extra work of an engaged course? Here, the rhetorical situation for students and teachers isn't satisfied with a wrangle over contradictions but calls for a probing rhetorical analysis of how to face those contradictions, go beyond mere advocacy, and make a difference. Moreover, it may need to put this collaborative inquiry into writing *and* into circulation—to create a public that pays attention.

Learning to negotiate such situations will require not just the transfer of writing skills but expansive and collaborative transformations. Even in familiar writing projects, the mentor and writer may be separated by not only race or class but peoples' aspirations and options for achieving them. And as we saw with the Decision Makers writers in Chapter 3, the personal relations between Scholar and Mentor were essential to putting concerns, uncertainty, limitations down on paper together, whether the issue was as public as a curfew policy or as personal as the experience of risk and respect. But the collaborative hill to climb isn't just letting someone be heard but helping them take on a new, demanding literate practice, by choice. This creates a challenging contact zone for both parties. Mentors must create a mutual awareness with their scholar that they are swimming up this new river together. And that may require taking on a literate practice not merely as a means to self-expression but putting writing to use in an unfamiliar civic context to call into being a new local public with one's words. In the Think Tank cases we observed in Chapters 2 and 3, literate practices such as collaborative planning and rivaling supported live interactions and drew writers into creating negotiated meanings. At the same time, I would say, collaboration was equally motivated and shaped by the looming presence of a live public performance before peers and strangers, coupled with the affirming prospect and intimidating expectations of an actual published, public text. This mix birthed a self-conscious recognition of being in a contact zone, of the value of difference, and of the need for negotiated understanding. Learning outcomes like these depend on immersing students as actors in the multiple dimensions of a live rhetorical problem and its space.

More generally, these complex contact zones showcase the way engaged education asks students to draw on rich conceptual frameworks for thinking about difference, conflict and difficult questions and to then put their current working hypothesis for negotiating them to the test of experience. When that powerful mix is coupled with metacognitive awareness of what you did, students are prepared to transform *this* learning in order to enter new, distinctive, and dynamic problem spaces.

Becoming a Grounded-Theory Builder

Just as choosing to analyze a rhetorical situation as an activity can broaden one's outward facing inquiry, grounded-theory building can heighten attunement to our own interpretations and actions. Working with this framework, students can begin to see themselves as agents with the power to translate their combination of course-based conceptual tools and experiential observation into a working theory—a hypothesis for action, rooted in and waiting to be tested by experience. For us, this means adapting the researcher's method of "grounded-practical-theory building" into a teachable practice designed for students.

The Nature of Grounded-Practical-Theory Building (GTB)

In their studies of "intellectual discussion in academic institutions," Robert Craig and Karen Tracy have translated grounded-theory building from sociology into a window on communication (248). They have given us a research method designed not only to describe but, as they argue, to build a *normative* theory which speaks directly to *practice*. Unlike an empirical description of what happened, its goal is a more prescriptive understanding, not unlike the ethical wisdom of Aristotle's phronesis. But here is the rub, as Craig and Tracy point out, theories "developed largely through philosophical speculation may be difficult to operationalize in practice or have little relevance to the problems and choices that practitioners typically experience" (250). The alternative, central to John Dewey's philosophical pragmatism as well, "envisions critical reflection not as a purely philosophical exercise external to practice, but as a process of inquiry that arises within practical situations in response to practical problems" (253). In grounded-practical-theory building, this means starting your inquiry at the ground level with people and situations— and then ferreting out, probing, and naming the problem that calls or spurs you to inquiry. Craig and Tracy call researchers to work toward a *normative* theory. However, I will suggest, when the "researchers" are students conducting their own engaged inquiry, we will want to adapt this powerful process to their lived contexts. Here, the goal of grounded-theory building will be better described as a hypothesis—a form of knowing open to experience I would call a "working theory."

Naming the Problem

In advocacy work, the problem may be readily apparent, as in contradictions between what a community or its students need and what its institutions are tooled up to provide. But as Heifetz' leadership cases show, our initial or a partisan assessment may not discern the deeper, less obvious problem, especially when that problem would require us to examine or even alter our own assumptions and predispositions (e.g., as we saw in the Community Think Tank featured in Chapter 3: aren't the difficulties of these "Independent" students' merely a matter of self-reliance or perhaps merely the indication of low effort?). As the writers in the hidden frames study of Chapter 4 revealed, the real problem may even be our own unrecognized marginalizing frames or image of our roles. In another example, Craig and Tracy's discourse analysis of troubled faculty communication practices revealed an ongoing conflict between their "situated ideals" or "inchoate normative principles" and the very techniques faculty relied on to address tensions that framed the problem (250). For instance, consider the difference between coming to a decision in an unstructured, opinion-airing faculty meeting or in a deliberative, problem-focused, problem-solving think tank roundtable. They go on to argue that the real function of a normative ideal may be to work as a counterfactual model used for "critically reflecting on practice that necessarily deviates from [this] norm"—that is, the ideal norm you are proposing (253). Yet it is important to note how in all these cases, actually naming the problem your theory would address can require research and extended critical inquiry.

The Work of Interpretation

Naming the problem is the initial step in the extended process of building a theory, which Paulo Freire describes as praxis or action/reflection. In a problem-oriented class, this might begin with reading, observation, and discussion as inquiry moves in a hermeneutic circle of pre-interpretation, action, critical reflection, reinterpretation, and further action. "'Theory' (conceptual thought) and 'practice' (situated action) can be understood as moments within this process" (Craig and Tracy 252).

In Aristotle's account, praxis is a way to create practical knowledge or wisdom, phronesis. Because this good judgment is often realized in situations of choice or deliberation, he highlights the role rhetorical skill or techné plays in the process of discovery. Likewise, in Craig and Tracy's account of building a normative model of communication, it takes both rhetorical insight and interaction to build a "rational reconstruction of practice" (248) that is both useful and a "morally and politically significant social practice" (252). The construction of a situated, useful normative theory of communication problems, they note, is most likely to emerge in the interactive discussions we see in "brown bags, seminars and colloquia and in arguments directed to educators, analysts, organizers" (255). How, then, shall we draw students in an engaged course beyond mere participation into this powerful work of interpretation?

For this purpose, grounded-theory building (GTB) offers a set of distinctive moves. It starts not with a topic or much less a claim but with intentional engagement with a problem, a conflict, or a contradiction. And instead of turning to prior theory or received wisdom, it initiates a problem analysis based on close observation. It probes not only the context but looks in particular for the strategies, practices, or techniques at play in this communication problem. Here is where GTB goes beyond standard research, as it seeks to construct an *ideal* or *normative practice*. The aim is practical wisdom, praxis, action. But there is one more twist in the road, because the ideals articulated in a *grounded*-practical theory must necessarily be *situated ideals*. They are not generalized, abstract principles but a reconstruction from the data of observation. What they offer is a "reasoned basis for the resolution of pragmatic dilemmas" (Craig and Tracy 259). Should we do X or Y?

In Craig and Tracy's framework, researchers are the agents and other faculty are the audience. Our task is to adapt it for students in community-engaged classes in which the challenge is not for educators to create grounded theories (unless it is about better teaching) but to offer students a new power tool for transforming their own knowledge guided by a metacognitive awareness of *themselves* as grounded-theory builders. The change would start with a role reversal in which the students are the researchers to whom we lend support. One approach to adapting comes out of a comparison Craig and Tracy make to other research. In one comment, they note many parallels to the early research John R. Hayes and I did on the cognitive processes of writers, particularly its focus on problems and close observation. Then, as they point out, since that research doesn't try to construct a normative goal, it offers no implications for action.

However, I would argue, a more accurate distinction, especially relevant to teaching, is that those writing studies were motivated by two complementary disciplinary goals. One was to build a data-based descriptive model of a cognitive process—a key move in cognitive psychology (Hayes). The other, however, was to use the observed differences between expert and novice writers as a guide to identifying and teaching some of the rhetorical problem-solving strategies on which experienced writers draw (Flower, *Problem-Solving*). In this sense, we were indeed reconstructing *these* observations into situated ideals. However, there is another important difference. Unlike a *normative* theory, such strategies are always heuristics—working hypotheses, merely high-probability moves, designed to give students a new awareness and conscious control of their own strategic choices. So the next step in our educational research, I would suggest, is to discover how best to teach this sort of strategic knowledge by observing what learners actually do with it in practice. In place of a normative theory, we would be working for a situated hypothesis subject to being tested and developed by experience.

Teaching Theory Builders

Let us consider an example of a student theory builder trying to make sense of a no doubt familiar intercultural encounter in a community literacy project. Keith, a white college mentor, wanted to understand what he called "productive frictions" within "circuits of power." He was also trying to minimize his power position in his relationship with Chandra, an African American teenager (often amused at his politicized reading of her day-to-day life). At the same time, he was trying to push her to rigorous thinking and to entice her to interrogate her own assumptions, just as he, a cultural studies student, did. Yet how did Chandra construe this experience and interpret its meaning? For his final paper, Keith was trying to build a scaffold for teaching about power relations. After documenting all the instances of the often-subtle shifts in power he observed between teens, mentors, and adults, his grounded theory was still trying to balance both the fluidity of the power dynamics at the CLC with one of his own "foiled attempts" to shift them. Connecting theory to the world of practice can be difficult.

A comparison with his graduate student mentor-coordinator will demonstrate a more extended practice of theory building that entertains even more demanding goals. Starting with a tool I have described as "observation-based theory building," this way of conducting research in writing and reading combines the tools of educational research with the agenda of feminist science. As Donna Haraway describes the goal of research: "Feminists have to insist on a project . . . that offers a more adequate, richer, better account of the world, in order to live in it well (Haraway, qtd. in Flower, "Observation" 167).

But Haraway's agenda also adds two additionally rigorous demands. The first is an ethical stance to conduct this inquiry "in critical reflexive relation to our own as well as others' practices of domination and the unequal part of privilege and oppression that make up all positions" (167). The second is an epistemological stance which recognizes that, since all knowledge is situated knowledge, alternative explanations can co-exist. Yet at the same time, this agenda seeks to build "no-nonsense commitments to faithful accounts of the 'real world'" that go beyond critique—to develop what Donna Haraway would call "feminist objectivity." As Sandra Harding puts it, in the place of making personal position statements much less Truth claims, we are engaged in the rhetorical process of case building in order to offer "reliable grounds for deciding just which claims to knowledge are preferable" (qtd. in Flower, "Observation" 167).

Here our theory builder Elenore Long (clearly not just any mentor) was using her dissertation to build just such a "case" by asking, "how do we negotiate intercultural images of literacy?" In a preview of work to come, her observation-based theory building, like grounded theory, had started with probing and analyzing this problem, observing on many levels, and recording multiple kinds of data. And with this observational grounding, she began to forge links with academic reading, research, and her own intuitions and hypotheses, drawing on conceptual tools ranging from close analysis, to articulating rival hypotheses, to submitting her coding to reliability checks and tests of probability. All of which led her back in turn to the data and new possibilities. In short, she was building a researcher's negotiated meaning (Long "The Rhetoric").[3] As an observation-based theory builder, she was working. on the one hand, to create "a meaningful *interpretation* of the world; and,

---

3. Long's study, initially subtitled "The Rhetoric of Social Action: College Mentors Negotiating Intercultural Images of Literacy" appeared in 2000 in Inventing *a Discipline* (edited by Maureen Goggin) which traces the formative years of Rhetoric and Composition as a discipline. What stands out there is the way *teaching* writing was the dynamic force in the discipline's new theory building.

on the other, to *test that constructed reality* in clear and careful ways against the rich and contrary data of experience" (Flower, "Observation" 183).[4]

It is not surprising that as a graduate student, Elenore Long was acutely aware of herself as a grounded-theory builder, aware of her methods, and the unknowns she was working with. Examples of the transformative work that followed have turned up in previous chapters. But what would it take for an *undergraduate* mentor to see this sequence of reading, contact, discussion and writing as pieces of the frame in their own process of building (rebuilding) a grounded theory? How could a socially engaged course make them aware of their own agency, taking them beyond a mere response, into an ongoing process of critical interpretation, to be tested by experience, then shaped and even transformed in the face of new problems that emerge (that will perhaps call for new grounded working theories)? Moreover, how do you lay a foundation for the even more independent work of transformation? Based on these case studies (as we saw in Chapters 2 and 3) I will argue that one of the most powerful underlying forces that both instigates and guides transformation is a student's metacognitive awareness of what they have learned and its significance. Such awareness develops naturally over time, but let us consider what we mean by the term and how our teaching might set this in motion.

The Nature of Metacognitive Awareness

Imagine for a moment the understanding your own metacognitive awareness might create in a situation like this. Chad, a Pittsburgh urban teenager, had just written a forceful argument against his school's ineffectual suspension practice, with lively interpolated street language for effect, which would soon be published in one of the Community Literacy Center's widely circulated newsletters. His teacher comes up to you at the public Community Conversation where the teenagers are presenting their writing and dramatizing their ideas. In an annoyed, dismissive tone, she informs you, "You are undoing all my work—telling him that he can *write*!" How should you respond? Suppressing your immediate (quite undiplomatic reaction), you take a mental step back to ask yourself: How should I even interpret this interaction? What is the *real* problem here? What would the probable effects of alternative emotional, rational, or inquiring responses be? And perhaps later, as you engage in metacognitive reflection on your own thoughts: Why did I respond the way I did? Does this information have any implications for my mentoring, teaching, interaction with the schools? How would you respond? To what purpose?

---

4. I would also like to note that the paper quoted here carried a footnote thanking a number of colleagues whose ideas and voices helped make it. What should be added to its account of observation-based theory building goes beyond mere appreciation of these valued individuals to a more sophisticated understanding of the highly significant, constructive role a whole network of colleagues plays in shaping and improving any attempt at theory building. An omission I would like to rectify if I could. Research is a highly collaborative experience.

"Metacognition" like "transfer" is a promiscuous term used for different activities and multiple levels of consciousness as noted in Chapter 5. In the research on the regulation of learning, its multiple facets include various metacognitive acts, from responses at the level of unconscious processing to conscious deliberation and the regulation of cognition. The unconscious activity kicks in, for instance, when comprehension of a sentence stumbles and a reader automatically goes back to reread the problematic sentence. But at the level of conscious observation and reflection, the reader may pause to ask, "Why is this confusing?" Or the reader may draw on a strategy, like recalling the context; or may consider a plan to solve the dilemma, such as asking in class; or may go so far as to notice how their own speed-reading practice may not be working so well here. And some readers may make the even more demanding cognitive move of drawing a connecting inference or venturing an explanation for this experience (e.g., *is this problem with me or something about this text?*). The examples of transformation in this book are chosen to reflect this higher-level metacognitive work. As we saw in the cases, metacognition might take the form of a focused memory search, probing one's thinking, assumptions, and experiences; and it can even rise to articulating not only remembered events, but the feelings and judgments they engendered. As in my encounter with that high school teacher, this can allow a more revealing comparison of one's initial cognitive and affective response to one's own current interpretation. Metacognition can stage an internal mental drama.

In rhetoric and composition, we assign reflection for many purposes, from prompting a review of assigned readings to revising one's own writing. For our purposes, I wish to focus on a distinctive form of reflection designed to support that higher level of metacognitive awareness that feeds and invites transformation. Given that engaged education, by its very nature, seeks to adapt to its setting, I cannot presume to offer the practices, much less curriculum, that might be best for yours. For example, prompting such reflection is itself a very opportunistic move: it can happen in a conversation walking down the hall, in a debriefing, or in dedicated class discussions on the formal assignments as described in Chapter 5. More importantly, although this book does offer descriptions of some practices I and others have worked with, that may or may not be suited to your goals. However, we can look at our own assignments, practices, and goals to gauge how directly they support students' own awareness. And to note how we do it: through invitation, modeling, scaffolding . . . ?

Three Tests for Teaching Metacognitive Awareness

Like activity analysis, grounded-theory building is a rhetorical theory *and* a practice we are likely to be good at teaching, focused as it is on observing, naming and interpreting a live and present problem. Metacognition is the next step to actually *becoming* a theory builder. However, this power tool is a highly individual, internal action—a form of awareness that is hard to model or observe. So I would like to conclude this chapter, first by sketching a set of tests teachers can use to ask: do I see any evidence that my students are building bridges, seeing applications, and making change. And secondly, to offer a Guide for students to help them ask these critical questions for themselves, in a collaborative inquiry with others.

1. The Bridge test.

How does a given practice (in a course or on site) help students build bridges that go from their academic/intellectual work to their experiential realities and then to reflective interpretations? Have they been able to articulate the connections, the disjunctions, the contradictions, insights, the opportunities that drawing these inferences can reveal? Bear in mind, building real bridges takes time, tools, and effort.

2. The Application test.

Many of the passionately held ideas we have discussed here—from philosophical pragmatism, engaged education, public deliberation, community engaged writing and rhetoric to building grounded theories—have at their core concerns for social action, interaction, being useful, making change, and their consequences. But in the humanities, school is not always designed to teach, promote, track or sometimes even care about the application and outcomes of what students learned. So, we might ask whether or not our given educational practice is asking students to go beyond the experience of being immersed in an activity to consider an application of what they have learned beyond this horizon. Notice, as a foundation for transforming knowledge, this is asking what they have *taught themselves*. As we have seen in Chapters 2 and 5, for some students the new application turned up in other courses, in their professional plans as a writer, engineer, economist, or in decisions in family business. For others it informed their role in other community connections, in political or social activism, even in their sense of identity.

An educational practice supporting *application* would invite students to extend that *bridge* built from theory, to experience, to reflective interpretation, on out into the unknown. However, these are still students, in a course, not reviewing options in the career planning office. This educational practice calls, first, for real thinking, uncovering applications of an idea, drawing inferences, seeing the connection to problems, imagination. It is genuinely constructive work. And secondly, to go beyond a thought exercise, as useful as one may be, in Chapter 4 we saw students using a written reflection on their *current application* of these ideas to raise consciousness of applying learning as an immediate, self-conscious move. It had never occurred to Justine—Chapter 4—that teaching argument involved more than adversarial debate. The test here is whether a given teaching practice is supporting a new metacognitive awareness of the choices a given application entails for themselves and others, the assumptions they are working from, and the consequences of acting.

3. The Discovery and Change Test

This attention to application has an equally distinguished background in both rhetoric and liberatory education. One of the founding voices of contemporary rhetoric and composition, Richard E. Young, captured this approach with his book title: *Rhetoric: Discovery and Change*. Unlike classical studies or communication's focus on argument or persuasion, this rhetoric reimagined the ancient art of *Invention*, which put the art of meaning making at the heart of what writers do. In doing so it celebrated the power of writing itself as first of all an act of discovery *for the writer*. How then do our students perceive their own acts of written meaning making, beyond the production of a text? Are they thinking about their thinking?

I am (well, was) in fact working out what I wanted to I mean here while walking down a deeply wooded trail, stopping to jot down alternative sentence bits on this scrap of paper, all the while attending to the sheer exuberance of low spring plants, shaded by towering trees, sheltering some insistently courting bird calls around me. And in the next instant, I began attending to the steady stream of ideas, connections, memories, and all the words that began to pop up as fresh possibilities that could create or support (somehow, but just how exactly?) this idea of "Discovery and Change." Soon I was also thinking about thinking, about how all this was being brought into consciousness, to be worked with, by that willful act of writing. (And I should note, words to be again revised as I finish this manuscript.)

Pace Coleridge's myth of inspiration, I would *not* say, even in this meditative space, that all this rose up before me "with a parallel production of correspondent expression, without any sensation or consciousness of effort."[5] This is not to say that inspiration isn't real and amazingly productive, but it is unlikely to do the work we have in mind that can actually build bridges into unknown territory and construct the inferences that envision and test their applications. Rather than merely putting an intact meaning into words, this kind of writing is often an extended constructive process of figuring out what inchoate felt connections could actually mean, drawing new inferences, challenging old ones, testing it against the words we do have. And it helps to realize all this is a normal process.

Let me shift to another discourse (often a revealing tool for invention). In teaching for metacognitive awareness, we are inviting students to turn their yet-to-be-connected pockets of "knowing" into an articulated form. That will include first exploring disparate parts of one's memory networks (some salient or accessible, some not), then translating multiple mental representations (some visual, others affective, propositional, as well as linguistic) into words. And the language itself may still be writer-based, ill-considered, or vague, lacking the nuanced complexity of a sophisticated representation (Flower, "Images"). And as expert/novice studies suggest, experienced writers go well beyond an expressive utterance to building an actively negotiated meaning (Flower, *Construction; Writer-Based*).

---

5. This account of composing Kubla Khan turned out, in fact, to be quite fictitious.

Echoing the value of awareness, Paulo Freire's liberatory "problem-posing education" describes the central goal as achieving "critical consciousness"—learning to perceive social contradictions and take action against oppression (19). And like Richard Young, in the test he proposes learners would combine the rhetoric of articulated discovery with metacognitive *awareness* to carry out the purposeful work of *change*. As Freire puts it, "to exist, humanly, is to *name* the world, to change it. Once named, the world in its turn reappears to the namers as a problem and requires of them a new naming. Men are not built in silence, but in word, in work, in action-reflection" (88).

This test looks at our students' metacognitive awareness of their own writing as a process of Discovery and Change. Such an agenda adapts grounded observation and theory building for an explicit purpose—for action, for making change, and for the pragmatist's search for outcomes. The consequential vision of John Dewey and the prophetic pragmatism of Cornel West that shaped my understanding of intercultural inquiry speak directly to this larger project of locating the educational power of community engagement in its outcomes (Flower, *Community*). Dewey would move us from forming hypotheses to the ongoing critical search which locates the meaning of this hypothesis in outcomes. The value of our conceptions is determined "by the consequences they effect in existence as it is perceptibly experienced" (Quest 132). West adds the ethical imperative to probe experiential consequences for the most marginalized. This interaction is eloquently captured by Rachel Shah: "West's deep and soulful stance against injustice adds a necessary analysis of power to Dewey's emphasis on experiential knowledge, antifoundational questioning, and feet-on-the-ground commitment to action" (17). I would ask, are my students aware of the power of or reflecting on their own process of "discovery and change."

Supporting Grounded-Theory Actors

As a teacher I have found these three tests of engaged education helpful. But at this point it is appropriate to turn the inquiry over to students: to shift from the tests of our curriculum to students' reflection on their own in-process theory building and its bridge to action. As people become self-conscious agents of their own learning, the opportunity to compare their developing understanding and uncertainties with one another can open up both possibilities and useful problems. The following collaborative tool is written for students to use to test their own progress in the same three curriculum areas we have been considering above: building *bridges,* envisioning *applications,* and linking *discovery to change*. The questions are designed to help them prepare for a more in-depth discussion with colleagues (in the class and community) of their problem-oriented "theory-in-progress."[6]

---

6. The notion of sharing our thinking, hypotheses, learning with our community partners is an important step from service to collaboration. One of the best, and very grounded, guides to this is found in Rachael Shah's *Rewriting Partnerships*.

What Is Your Grounded Theory Saying Today? A Preparation for Making Thinking Visible

As a grounded-theory builder, use these questions to prepare for a collaborative discussion by asking yourself, "How would I explain this to myself, or to someone else who asks me to." As a Collaborative Planning Partner in the role of Supporter, prepare to ask these probing questions and help your Partner take the inquiry deeper.

1. Entering into Engagement

1. Community engaged courses take people into a new world and an unfamiliar, complex *activity system*. How would you compare what you expected to what you found?
2. You probably ran into or noticed a couple of *problems*. How did you interpret them?
3. How did you *respond*?
4. So, what did you conclude or *learn* from that experience?
5. Can you think of any *rivals* to how you named the problem or chose to act?

2. Reading the Situation

1. Whenever writing or speaking is involved, you are in a rhetorical situation. How did you *read* the rhetorical situation you found yourself in, especially when you looked at it as part of a larger activity?
2. Did you have to *interact* with any institutions, traditions, or rules? How so?
3. Were you aware of the *roles* you and other people were supposed to play? Or of your place in a *hierarchy* with relations based on status or power? How did you *respond* to that situation?
4. Did you ever need to switch from one *Discourse* to another? If you weren't already an "insider" in one of those Discourses, how did you respond?
5. Did you find yourself drawing on any particularly useful *tools*? They could be material ones, such as technology, scheduled planning sessions, taking notes. Or conceptual ones, such as taking an inquiry stance in an intercultural contact zone, deliberately seeking out rival hypotheses, or methods you have learned for political, social, cultural, or cognitive analysis.
6. Activity systems are usually full of buried *contradictions* and ill-defined *conflicts*. As these areas are often the best sites for change, did you uncover any?
7. How did you define the problem—and its rivals?

8. What did you do in *response* (ignore it, describe it, discuss it, propose action, imagine consequences, or act)?

3. Collaborating in a Contact Zone

1. Community engagement will put us in contact with some significant differences. Thinking of your community partner, what have been the two or three most important differences for you? Don't rest with obvious ones like race, gender, orientation . . . Also consider barriers such as background, attitudes, assumptions, goals, and valuable differences in experiential knowledge, insight, and skills.
2. Was there something you had to work on together where these differences could matter? How so? Were they surprising, confusing, problematic, useful?
3. When you tried to collaborate and needed to negotiate your differences, did you hit a problem? How did you try to deal with it? And if you successfully worked something out, how did you do so?
4. What would you say you learned?

4. Becoming a Grounded-Theory Actor

1. Back when you first compared what you expected with what you found, you started building a personal interpretation or "theory" of the situation. As you moved to building your own more in-depth, *practical grounded theory*, what did you decide to focus on or try to understand?
2. More specifically, how would you define the meaningful *problem* with which you hope to engage? Think of it as a revealing conflict or one of those contradictions that frequently occur between two assumptions, practices, or forces that make a difference.
3. How many ways (tools) have you found to closely observe and document this problem in action?
4. What are some rival interpretations you have considered? And what are the consequences those ways of seeing your problem might have in *this situation*?
5. When you consider ways to respond to your problem, how would you meet the demands for a morally, socially, or politically significant practice?
6. Does your response name explicit, practical strategies for change?
7. Effective grounded-practical-theory builders are also observing and reflecting on their own learning and thinking, on their growing repertoire of strategies, and on their ways of dealing with conflict. Looking back at your own thinking in this project so far, what problems did you encounter, and what have you taught yourself?
8. So, what will you do now?

Works Cited

Adler-Kassner, Linda. "Because Writing is Never Just Writing." *College Composition and Communication,* vol. 69, no. 2, 2017, pp. 317–340.

Adler-Kassner, Linda, et al. "Service-Learning and Composition at the Crossroads." *Writing the Community: Concepts and Models for Service-Learning in Composition,* edited by Linda Adler-Kassner, et al. Taylor and Francis, 2023.

Adler-Kassner, Linda, and Peggy O'Neill. Reframing Writing Assessment to Improve Teaching *and Learning.* Utah State UP, 2010.

Alexander, Jonathan, et al. "Toward Wayfinding: A Metaphor for Understanding Writing Experiences." *Written Communication,* vol. 37, no. 1, 2020, pp. 104–31. https://doi.org/10.1177/0741088319882325.

Anderson, Richard C. "The Notion of Schemata and the Educational Enterprise." *Schooling and the Acquisition of Knowledge,* edited by Richard C Anderson et al., Lawrence Erlbaum Associates, 1977, pp. 415–41.

Anson, Chris M. "The Pop Warner Chronicles: A Case Study in Contextual Adaptation and the Transfer of Writing Ability." *College Composition and Communication,* vol. 67, no. 4, 2016, pp. 518–49. https://www.jstor.org/stable/44783545.

Asen, Robert. "Critical Engagement through Public Sphere Scholarship." *Quarterly Journal of Speech,* vol. 101, no. 1, 2015, pp. 132–44. https://doi.org/10.1080/00335630.2015.999983.

Atwill, Janet. *Rhetoric Reclaimed: Aristotle and the Liberal Arts Tradition.* Cornell UP, 1998.

Baird, Neil, and Bradley Dilger. "How Students Perceive Transitions: Dispositions and Transfer in Internships." *College Composition and Communication,* vol. 68, no. 4, 2017, pp. 684–712. https://www.jstor.org/stable/44783589.

Baker-Bell, April, et al. "This Ain't Another Statement! This is a DEMAND for Black Linguistic Justice!" *Conference on College Composition and Communication,* July 2020, cccc.ncte.org/cccc/demand-for-black-linguistic-justice.

Barouch, Timothy, and Brett Ommen. "The Constrained Liberty of the Liberal Arts and Rhetorical Education." *Rhetoric Society Quarterly,* vol. 47, no. 2, 2017, pp. 158–79. https://doi.org/10.1080/02773945.2016.1242767.

Bassok, Miriam, and Keith J. Holyoak. "Pragmatic Knowledge and Conceptual Structure: Determinants of Transfer Between Quantitative Domains." *Transfer on Trial: Intelligence, Cognition and Instruction,* edited by Douglas K. Detterman and Robert J. Sternberg, Alex Publishing, 1996, pp. 68–98.

Beach, King. "Consequential Transitions: A Sociocultural Expedition Beyond Transfer in Education." *Review of Research in Education,* vol. 24, no. 1, 1999, pp. 101–39. https://doi.org/10.3102/0091732X024001101.

Beaufort, Anne. *College Writing and Beyond: A New Framework for University Writing Instruction.* Utah State UP, 2007.

———. "Reflection: The Metacognitive Move towards Transfer of Learning." *A Rhetoric of Reflection,* edited by Kathleen Blake Yancey, Utah State UP, 2016, pp. 23–41.

Benford, Robert D., and David A. Snow. "Framing Processes and Social Movements: An Overview and Assessment." *Annual Review of Sociology*, vol. 26, 2000, pp. 611–39. https://www.jstor.org/stable/223459.

Bennett, Julia, et al. "Self-Advocacy." *Community Think Tank Findings*, 2018, www.cmu.edu/thinktank. Accessed 18 June 2023.

Bereiter, Carl, and Marlene Scardamalia. "From Conversation to Composition: The Role of Instruction in a Developmental Process." *Advances in Instructional Psychology*, vol. 2, edited by Robert Glaser, Lawrence Erlbaum, 1982, pp. 1–64.

———. "Knowledge Telling and the Problem of 'Inert' Knowledge." *The Psychology of Written Composition*, Lawrence Erlbaum, 1987, pp. 179–89.

Bitzer, Lloyd. "Political Rhetoric." *Landmark Essays on Contemporary Rhetoric*, edited by Thomas B. Farrell, Hermagoras, 1998, pp. 1–22.

———. "The Rhetorical Situation." *Philosophy and Rhetoric*, vol. 1, 1968, pp. 1–14.

Blakeslee, Ann M., et al. "Story of a Community-Based Writing Resource-And a Call to Engage." *Communication Design Quarterly Review*, vol. 11, no. 3, 2023, pp. 42–53. https://doi.org/10.1145/3592367.3592372.

Bonilla-Silva, Eduardo. *Racism without Racists: Color-Blind Racism and the Persistence of Racial Inequality in the United States*. Rowman & Littlefield, 2006.

Bosmajian, Haig A. "The Language of White Racism." *College English*, vol. 31, no. 3, 1969, pp. 263–72.

Boyer, Ernest L. and Arthur Levine. *A quest for common learning: The aims of general education*. The Carnegie Foundation for the Advancement of Teaching, 1981.

Boyle, Casey. "Writing and Rhetoric and/as Posthuman Practice." *College English*, vol. 78, no. 6, 2016, pp. 253–554. https://www.jstor.org/stable/44075143.

Bradley, L. Richard. "Evaluating Service-Learning: Toward a New Paradigm." *Service-Learning: Applications from the Research*, edited by Alan S. Waterman, Routledge, 1997, pp. 151–78.

Branson, Tyler S., et. al. "Collaborative Ecologies of Emergent Assessment: Challenges and Benefits Linked to a Writing-Based Institutional Partnership." *College Composition and Communication*, vol. 69, no. 2, 2017, pp. 287–316. https://www.jstor.org/stable/44783616.

Brent, Doug. "Crossing Boundaries: Co-Op Students Relearning to Write." *College Composition and Communication*, vol. 63, no. 4, 2012, pp. 558–92. https://www.jstor.org/stable/23264229.

Brown, Adrienne Maree. *Emergent strategy: Shaping change, shaping worlds*. AK Press, 2017.

Brown, Ann. L., and Annemarie Sullivan Palincsar. "Reciprocal Teaching of Comprehension Strategies: A Natural History for Enhancing Language." *Intelligence and Cognition in Special Children: Comparative Studies of Giftedness, Mental Retardation & Learning Disabilities*, edited by John Borkowski and Jeanne D. Day, Ablex, 1987, pp.81–132.

Castillo, Christopher. "Review: Community Is the Way: Engaged Writing and Designing for Transformative." *Reflections*, vol. 22, no. 2, spring, 2023, pp. 152–55. https://reflectionsjournal.net/2023/06/review-community-is-the-way-engaged-writing-and-designing-for-transformative-changereview/.

Chittum, Jessica R., et al. *The effects of community-based and civic engagement in higher education*. American Association of Colleges and Universities, 2022.

Cintron, Ralph. *Angels' Town: Chero Ways, Gang Life, and Rhetorics of the Everyday*. Beacon Press, 1997.

CMU Community Think Tank. *Carnegie Mellon University*, 22 April 2024, https://www.cmu.edu/thinktank.

Clifton, Jennifer. *Argument as Dialogue Across Difference: Engaging Youth in Public Literacies*. Routledge, Taylor & Francis Group, 2017.

Cloud, Dana L. *Reality Bites: Rhetoric and the Circulation of Truth Claims in U.S. Political Culture*. The Ohio State UP, 2018.

Cloud, Doug. *Arguing Identity and Human Rights: Among Rival Options*. Routledge, 2024.

———. "The Rise of the Gay Warrior: Rhetorical Archetypes and the Transformation of Identity." *Discourse & Communication*, vol. 13, 2019, pp. 26–47. https://doi.org/10.1177/1750481318801626.

Commer, Carolyn. *Championing a Public Good: A Call to Advocate for Higher Education*. Pennsylvania State UP, 2024.

———. *Shaping Education Policy in the Era of Neoliberal Reform: Lessons from the 2006 Spellings Commission Controversy*. 2016. Carnegie Mellon U, PhD dissertation.

Cone, James H. *Martin & Malcolm & America: A Dream or a Nightmare*. Orbis Books, 1991.

Coogan, David. *Writing Our Way Out: Memoirs from Jail*. Brandylane, 2016.

———. "Service Learning and Social Change: The Case for Materialist Rhetoric." *College Composition and Communication*, vol. 57, no. 4, 2006, pp. 667–93. https://www.jstor.org/stable/20456912.

Craig, Robert T., and Karen Tracy. "Grounded Practical Theory: The Case of Intellectual Discussion." *Communication Theory*, vol. 5, no. 3, 1995, pp. 248–72. https://doi.org/10.1111/j.1468-2885.1995.tb00108.x.

Crick, Nathan. "Composing the Will to Power: John Dewey on Democratic Rhetorical Education." *Rhetoric Society Quarterly*, vol. 46, no. 4, 2016, pp. 287–307. https://doi.org/10.1080/02773945.2016.1198964.

Cross, Robert L., and Andrew Parker. *The Hidden Power of Social Networks: Understanding How Work Really Gets Done in Organizations*. Harvard Business School Press, 2004.

Cushman, Ellen. "Wampum, Sequoyan, and Story: Decolonizing the Digital Archive." *College English*, vol. 76, no. 2, 2013, pp. 115–35. https://www.jstor.org/stable/24238145.

Deans, Tom. *Writing Partnerships: Service-Learning in Composition*. National Council of Teachers of English, 2000.

Decision Makers. Carnegie Mellon University, 22 April 2024, http://www.hss.cmu.edu/departments/english/muffin/sos/index.php.

Detterman, Douglas K., and Robert J. Sternberg, editors. *Transfer on Trial: Intelligence, Cognition, and Instruction*. Praeger, 1993.

Detweiler, J., et al. "Academic Leadership and Advocacy: On Not Leaning In." *College English*, vol. 79, no. 5, 2017, pp. 451–65. https://doi.org/10.58680/ce201729047.

Dewey, John. "Ethical Principles Underlying Education." *John Dewey on Education: Selected Writings*, edited by Reginald D. Archambault, U of Chicago P, 1974.

———. "The Nature of Aims." *John Dewey on Education: Selected Writings*, edited by Reginald Archambault. U of Chicago P, 1974, pp. 70–80.

———. *The Public and Its Problems*. Swallow, 1954.

———. *The Quest for Certainty. John Dewey: The Later Works, 1925–1953*, vol. 4, edited by Jo Ann Boydston, Southern Illinois UP, 1988.

Efklides, Anastasia. "How Does Metacognition Contribute to the Regulation of Learning? An Integrative Approach." *Psychological Topics*, vol. 23, no. 1, 2014, pp. 1–30.

Engeström, Yrjö. "Activity Theory and Individual and Social Transformation." *Perspectives on Activity Theory*, edited by Yrjö Engeström et al., Cambridge UP, 1999, pp. 19–38.

———. "Developmental Studies of Work as a Testbench of Activity Theory: Analyzing the Work of General Practitioners." *Understanding Practice: Perspectives on Activity and Context*, edited by Seth Chaiklin and Jean Lave, Cambridge UP, 1993, pp. 64–103.

———. "Innovative Learning in Work Teams: Analyzing Cycles of Knowledge Creation in Practice." *Perspectives on Activity Theory*, edited by Yrjö Engeström et al., Cambridge UP, 1999, pp. 378–405.

———. "Introduction." *Perspectives on Activity Theory*, edited by Yrjö Engeström et al., Cambridge UP, 1999, pp. 1–14.

———. *Learning by Expanding: An Activity-Theoretical Approach to Developmental Research*. Cambridge UP, 1987.

———. "Teachers as Collaborative Thinkers: Activity-Theoretical Study of an Innovative Teacher Team." *Teachers' Minds and Actions: Research on Teachers' Thinking and Practice*, edited by Ingrid Carlgren et al., The Falmer Press, 1994, pp. 45–63.

———. "Tensions of Judging: Handling Cases of Driving Under the Influence of Alcohol in Finland and California." *Cognition and Communication at Work*. Cambridge UP, 1996, pp. 200–33

Fine, Gary Alan, and Brooke Harrington. "Tiny Publics: Small Groups and Civil Society." *Sociological Theory*, vol. 22, no. 3, 2004, pp. 341–56. https://doi.org/10.1111/j.0735-2751.2004.00223.x.

Fischer, Frank. *Reframing Public Policy: Discursive Politics and Deliberative Practices*. Oxford UP, 2003.

Flanagan, John C. "The Critical Incident Technique." *Psychological Bulletin*, vol. 51, no. 4, 1954, pp. 327–58.

Flaxman, Erwin, and Margaret Orr. "Determining the Effectiveness of Youth Programs. ERIC/CUE Digest No. 118." *ERIC Clearinghouse on Urban Education*, 1996, pp. 1–9. https://files.eric.ed.gov/fulltext/ED412297.pdf.

Flower, Linda. *Community Literacy and the Rhetoric of Public Engagement*. U of Southern Illinois P, 2009.

———. *The Construction of Negotiated Meaning: A Social Cognitive Theory of Writing*. Southern Illinois UP, 1994.

———. "Difference-Driven Inquiry: A Working Theory of Local Public Deliberation." *Rhetoric Society Quarterly*, vol. 46, no. 4, 2016, pp. 308–40. https://doi.org/10.1080/02773945.2016.1194451.

———, editor. "Negotiating the Culture of Work and Technology." *Community Think Tank Findings*. https://www.cmu.edu/dietrich/english/courses/course-web pages/community-think-tank/ctt-files/23.pdf.

———, editor. "Healthcare: The Dilemma of Teamwork, Time and Turnover". https://www.cmu.edu/dietrich/english/courses/course-webpages/community-think-tank/ctt-files/healthcarefindings.pdf, 2002, pp. 1–7.

———. "Going Public—In a Disabling Discourse." *The Public Work of Rhetoric: Citizen-Scholars and Civic Engagement*, edited by John Ackerman and David Coogan, U of South Carolina P, 2010, pp. 137–15.

———. "Hidden Frames: Writing a Road to Change." *College Composition and Communication*, vol. 73, no. 1, 2021, pp. 27–51. https://doi.org/10.58680/ccc202131586.

———. "Intercultural Knowledge Building: The Literate Action of a Community Think Tank." *Writing Selves/Writing Societies: Research from Activity Perspectives*, edited by Charles Bazerman and David R. Russell, The WAC Clearinghouse/UP of Colorado, 2002, pp. 239–79. https://doi.org/10.37514/per-b.2003.2317.2.07.

———. "Observation-Based Theory Building. *Publishing in Rhetoric and Composition*, edited by Gary A. Olson and Todd W. Taylor, State U of New York P, 1997, pp. 163–85.

———. *Problem-Solving Strategies for Writing in College and Community*. Harcourt Brace College Publishers, 1998.

———. "Reflection: What Can Cognitive Rhetoric Offer Us?" *Contemporary Perspectives on Cognition and Writing*, edited by Patricia Portanova et al., The WAC Clearinghouse/UP of Colorado, 2017, pp. 331–45. https://doi.org/10.37514/per-b.2017.0032.3.2.

———. "Writer-Based Prose: A Cognitive Basis for Problems in Writing." *College English*, vol. 41, no. 1, 1979, pp.19–37.

Flower, Linda, and John R. Hayes. "Images, Plans and Prose: The Representation of Meaning in Writing." *Written Communication*, vol. 1, no. 1) 1984, pp. 120–160.

Flower, Linda, and Shirley Brice Heath. "Drawing on the Local: Collaboration and Community Expertise." *Language and Learning Across the Disciplines*, vol. 4, no. 3, 2000, pp. 43–55. https://doi.org/10.37514/LLD-J.2000.4.3.04.

Flower, Linda, et al. "Detection, Diagnosis, and the Strategies of Revision." *College Composition and Communication*, vol. 37, no. 1, 1986, pp. 16–55.

Flower, Linda, et al. *Learning to Rival: A Literate Practice for Intercultural Inquiry*. Lawrence Erlbaum, 2000.

Flower, Linda, et al. (Eds.). *Making Thinking Visible: Writing, Collaborative Planning, and Classroom Inquiry*. National Council of Teachers of English, 1994.

Flower, Linda, et al. *Reading-to-Write: Exploring a Cognitive and Social Process*. Oxford UP, 1990.

Freire, Paulo. *Pedagogy of the Oppressed*. 1968. Translated by M. B. Ramos, Continuum, 2005.

Gee, James Paul. "Literacy, Discourse, and Linguistics: Introduction and What is Literacy?" *Journal of Education*, vol. 171, no. 1, 1989, pp. 5–25. https://doi.org/10.1177/002205748917100101.

Glavan, Mary. *The Rhetoric of Situated Advocacy: Disability and the Price of Persuasion.* 2017. Carnegie Mellon University, PhD dissertation.

———. "Reframing Difference as Rhetorical Labor." In process.

Goffman, Erving. *Frame Analysis: An Essay on the Organization of Experience.* Harvard UP, 1974.

Goggin, Maureen Daly, editor. *Inventing a Discipline: Rhetoric: Scholarship in Honor of Richard E. Young,* National Council of Teachers of English, 2000.

Goldblatt, Eli. *Because We Live Here: Sponsoring Literacy Beyond the College Curriculum.* Hampton Press, 2007.

———. Symposium Organizer. Imagining Community Literacy. Invitational Symposium, Philadelphia PA, Temple University, April 18–21. 2008.

Goldblatt, Eli and David Jolliffe. *Literacy as Conversation: Learning Networks in Urban and Rural Communities.* U of Pittsburgh P, 2020.

Gott, Sherrie P., et al. "A Naturalistic Study of Transfer: Adaptive Expertise in Technical Domains." *Transfer on Trial: Intelligence, Cognition and Instruction*, edited by Douglas K. Detterman and Robert J. Sternberg, Alex Publishing, 1996, pp. 258–88.

Grabill, Jeffrey T. "On Being Useful: Rhetoric and the Work of Engagement." *The Public Work of Rhetoric: Citizen-Scholars and Civic Engagement*, edited by John M Ackerman and David J. Coogan, U of South Carolina P, 2013, pp. 193–210.

Gramsci, Antonio. *The Gramsci Reader: Selected Writings 1916–1935.* Forgacs, D. (Ed.). Q. Hoare & G. Nowell-Smith, Trans. New York UP. 1971/2000.

Grant, David M. "Review of Composition in the Age of Austerity, Nancy Welch and Tony Scott, Eds." *Kairos: A Journal of Rhetoric, Technology, and Pedagogy*, vol. 22, no. 2, 2018. https://kairos.technorhetoric.net/22.2/reviews/grant/index.html.

Greeno, James G., et al. "Transfer of Situated Learning." *Transfer on Trial: Intelligence, Cognition and Instruction*, edited by Douglas K. Detterman and Robert J. Sternberg, Alex Publishing, 1996, pp. 99–167.

Handley, Derek. *Struggle for the City: Rhetorics of Citizenship and Resistance during the Black Freedom Movement.* Penn State UP, 2024.

Harris, Joseph. "Negotiating the Contact Zone." *Journal of Basic Writing*, vol. 14, no. 1, 1995, pp. 27–42. https://doi.org/10.37514/JBW-J.1995.14.1.05.

Hartelius, E. Johanna. "Revisiting Vico's Pedagogy of Invention: The Intellectual Entrepreneurship Pre-Graduate School Internship." *Quarterly Journal of Speech*, vol. 98, no. 2, 2012, pp. 153–77. https://doi.org/10.1080/00335630.2012.663498.

Hauser, Gerald A. *Vernacular Voices: The Rhetoric of Publics and Public Spheres.* U of South Carolina P, 1999.

Hayes, John R. "Modeling and Remodeling Writing." *Written Communication*, vol. 29, no. 3, 2012, pp. 369–88. https://doi.org/10.1177/0741088312451260.

Heifetz, Ronald A. *Leadership Without Easy Answers.* Harvard UP, 1994.

Helberg, Alex. *Imagining the Political: The Role of Collective Persuasion in the Rhetoric of Social Movements.* 2021. Carnegie Mellon U, PhD dissertation.

Higgins, Lorraine, et al. "Community Literacy: A Rhetorical Model for Personal and Public Inquiry." *Community Literacy*, vol. 1, no. 1, 2006, pp. 9–43.

Hirschman, Albert O. "Social Conflicts as Pillars of Democratic Market Society." *Political Theory*, vol. 22, no. 2, 1994, pp. 203–18.

Holmes, Ashley J. *Public Pedagogy in Composition Studies*. National Council of Teachers of English, 2016.

Hull, Glynda, et al. "Remediation as Social Construct: Perspectives from an Analysis of Classroom Discourse." *College Composition and Communication*, vol. 42, no. 3, 1991, pp. 299–329.

Inoue, Asao B. *Antiracist Writing Assessment Ecologies*. The WAC Clearinghouse/Parlor Press, 2015. https://doi.org/10.37514/PER-B.2015.0698.

James, William. The Principles of Psychology. Harvard UP, 1983.

Johnson, Steven. *Farsighted: How We Make the Decisions That Matter the Most*. Riverhead Books, 2018.

Knight, Aimée. *Community Is the Way: Engaged Writing and Designing for Transformative Change*. The WAC Clearinghouse/UP of Colorado, 2022, https://doi.org/10.37514/pra-b.2022.1480.

Kolb, David A. *Experiential Learning: Experience as the Source of Learning and Development*. Prentice Hall, 1984.

Kuglitsch, Rebecca, and Lindsay M. Roberts. "*Scholarship of Teaching and Learning and Transfer of Information Literacy Skills*." University Libraries University of Colorado Boulder, 2019. https://scholar.colorado.edu/concern/book_chapters/4f16c3684.

Labov, William. *Language in the Inner City: Studies in Black English Vernacular*. U of Pennsylvania P, 1972.

Long, Elenore, *Community Literacy and the Rhetoric of Local Publics*. Parlor Press/The WAC Clearinghouse, 2008. https://wac.colostate.edu/books/referenceguides/long-community/.

———. *A Responsive Rhetorical Art: Artistic Methods for Contemporary Public Life*. U of Pittsburgh P, 2018.

———. "The Rhetoric of Social Action: College Mentors Inventing the Discipline." *Inventing a Discipline: Rhetoric Scholarship in Honor of Richard E. Young*, edited by M. Goggin, National Council of Teachers of English, 2000, pp. 289–318.

Lundgren, Henriette, and Rob F. Poell. "On critical reflection: A review of Mezirow's theory and its operationalization." *Human Resource Development Review*, vol. 15, no. 1, 2016, pp. 3–28. https://doi.org/10.1177/1534484315622735.

Martinez, Aja Y., *Counterstory: The Rhetoric of Writing and Critical Race Theory*. National Council of the Teachers of English, 2020.

Mathieu, Paula. *Tactics of Hope: The Public Turn in English Composition*. Boynton/Cook Heinemann, 2005.

McConnell, Kathleen F. "Imbalances and Inequities: The Structure of Inquiry and Its Place in Rhetorical Studies." *Rhetoric Society Quarterly*, vol. 45, no. 1, 2015, pp. 47–64. https://doi.org/10.1080/02773945.2014.980519.

Mehan, Hugh. "Beneath the Skin and the Ears: A Case Study in the Politics of Representation." *Understanding Practice: Perspectives on Activity and Context*, edited by Seth Chaiklin and Jean Lave, Cambridge UP, 1993, pp. 241–68.

Miller, Bruce A. "Service-Learning in Support of Rural Community Development." *Service-Learning: Applications from the Research*, edited by Alan S. Waterman, Routledge, 1997, pp. 107–26.

Miller, Thomas P., and Joddy Murray, eds. "Guest Editors' Introduction: Reimagining Leadership after the Public Turn." *College English*, vol. 79, no.5, 2017k, pp. 435–450. https://doi.org/10.58680/ce201729046.

Moore, Jessie. "Mapping the Questions: The State of Writing-Related Transfer Research." *Composition Forum*, vol. 26, 2012, pp. 1–13. https://compositionforum.com/issue/26/map-questions-transfer-research.php.

Moreau, Craig. "Teaching Students in the Technical and Professional Communication Classroom Practices for Innovation in Rhetoric." *Journal of Business and Technical Communication*, vol. 40, 2022, pp. 1–40. https://doi.org/10.1177/10506519221105495.

———. "Teams that Innovate: The Language of Difference-Driven Inquiry at the Workplace." *Business and Professional Communication Quarterly*, vol. 83, no. 4, 2020, pp. 385–408. https://doi.org/10.1177/2329490620949864.

Muhammad, Gholdy. *Unearthing Joy: A Guide to Culturally and Historically Responsive Teaching and Learning*. Scholastic, 2023.

Nowacek, Rebecca S. *Agents of Integration: Understanding Transfer as a Rhetorical Act*. Southern Illinois UP, 2011.

Paris, Scott, and Peter Winograd. "How Metacognition Can Promote Academic Learning and Instruction." *Dimensions of Thinking and Cognitive Instruction*, edited by Beau Fly Jones and Lorna Idol, Erlbaum, 1990, pp. 15–52.

Parks, Sharon Daloz. *Leadership Can Be Taught: A Bold Approach for a Complex World*. Harvard Business Review P, 2005.

Parks, Steve. "Sinners Welcome: The Limits of Rhetorical Agency." *College English*, vol. 76, no. 6, 2014, pp. 506–24. https://doi.org/10.58680/ce201425460.

———. "Strategic Speculations on the Question of Value: The Role of Community Publishing in English." *College English*, vol. 71, no. 5, 2009, pp. 506–27. https://www.jstor.org/stable/25652988.

Peck, Wayne C. *Community Advocacy: Composing for Action*. 1991. Carnegie Mellon U, PhD dissertation.

Peck, Wayne C., Linda Flower, and Lorraine Higgins. "Community Literacy." *College Composition and Communication*, vol. 46, no. 2, 1995, pp. 199–222. https://doi.org/10.58680/ccc19958743.

Perkins, D. N., and Gavriel Salomon. "Transfer and Teaching Thinking." *Thinking: The Second International Conference*, edited by D. N. Perkins et al., Erlbaum, 1987, pp. 285–303.

Paulus, Paul, and Huei-Chuan Yang. "Idea Generation in Groups: A Basis for Creativity in Organizations." *Organizational Behaviour and Human Decision Processes*, vol. 82, no. 1, May 2000, pp. 76–87. https://doi.org/10.1006/obhd.2000.2888.

Redd, Teresa, "In the Eye of the Beholder: Contrasting Views of Community Service Writing." *Reflections*, vol. 7, no. 9, 2003, pp. 15. https://reflectionsjournal.net/2020/05/in-the-eye-of-the-beholder-contrasting-views-of-community-service-writing-by-teresa-m-redd/.

Rein, Martin, and Donald Schon. "Reframing Policy Discourse." *The Argumentative Turn in Policy Analysis and Planning*, edited by Frank Fischer and John Forester, Duke UP, 1993, pp. 145–66.

Rivers, Nathaniel, and Ryan Weber. "Ecological, Pedagogical, Public Rhetoric." *College English*, vol. 63, no. 2, 2011, pp. 187–218. https://www.jstor.org/stable/23131582.

Roderick, Ryan. "Self-Regulation and Rhetorical Problem Solving: How Graduate Students Adapt to an Unfamiliar Writing Project." *Written Communication*, vol. 36, no. 3, 2019, pp. 410-36. https://doi.org/10.1177/0741088319843511.

Roderick, Ryan, and Craig Moreau. "Becoming a Scholar: Genre Knowledge, Self-regulation, and a Graduate Student's Transition from MA to PhD." *Writing & Pedagogy*, vol. 12, no. 1, 2020, pp. 157–183. https://doi.org/10.1558/wap.34586.

Rooney Andrea, et al. *Academic Teams: Engineering Capstone and Design Courses*. Carnegie Mellon, 2018, https://www.cmu.edu/dietrich/english/courses/course-webpages/community-think-tank/ctt-files/academic-teamwork-at-cmu.pdf.

Roozen, Kevin. "Reflective Interviewing." *A Rhetoric of Reflection*, edited by Kathleen Blake Yancey, Utah State UP, 2016, pp. 250–67.

Rousculp, Tiffany. "When the Community Writes: Re-Envisioning the SLCC DiverseCity Writing Series." *Reflections*, vol. 5, no. 1, 2006, pp. 67–88. https://reflectionsjournal.net/wp-content/uploads/2019/12/V5.N1.Rousculp.Tiffany.pdf.

Russell, David R. "Uses of Activity Theory in Written Communication Research." *Learning and Expanding with Activity Theory*, edited by Annalisa Sannino et al., Cambridge UP, 2009, pp. 40–52.

Ryder, Phyllis. "Public 2.0 Social Networking, Non-profits, and the Rhetorical Work of Public Making." *Reflections*, vol. 10, no. 1, 2010, pp. 229–56. https://reflectionsjournal.net/wp-content/uploads/2011/02/V10.N1.Ryder_.Phylliss.pdf.

———. *Rhetorics for Community Action: Public Writing and Writing Publics*. Lexington Books, 2011

Sannino, Annalisa. "Teachers Talk of Experiencing: Conflict, Resistance and Agency." *Teaching and Teacher Education*, vol. 26, 2010, pp. 838–44 https://doi.org/10.1016/j.tate.2009.10.021.

Schaffer, Marjorie, and Carol Hargate, "Moving Toward Reconciliation: Community Engagement in Nursing Education." *Journal of Community Engagement and Scholarship*, vol. 8, no. 1, 2015, pp. 60–68. https://doi.org/10.54656/PFQK9362.

Scardamalia, Marlene, and Carl Bereiter. "Knowledge Telling and Knowledge Transforming in Written Composition." *Advances in Applied Psycholinguistics, Vol. 2: Reading, Writing, and Language Learning*, edited by Sheldon Rosenberg, Cambridge UP, 1987, pp. 142–75.

Schutz, Aaron, and Anne Ruggles Gere. "Service Learning and English Studies: Rethinking 'Public' Service." *College English*, vol. 60, no. 2, 1998, pp. 129–49. https://doi.org/10.58680/ce19983675.

Scott, Tony. "Subverting Crisis in the Political Economy of Composition." *College Composition and Communication*, vol. 68, no. 1, 2016, pp. 10–37. https://www.jstor.org/stable/44783525.

Shah, Rachael W. *Rewriting Partnerships Community Perspectives on Community-Based Learning*. Utah State UP, 2020.

Smitherman, Geneva. *Talkin' and Testifyin': The Language of Black America*. Houghton Mifflin, 1977.

Stack, Garret, and Linda Flower. "Negotiating Knowledge and Advocating Change: Teaching for Transformative Practice." *Environmental Communication Pedagogy and Practice*, edited by Tema Milstein and Mairi Pileggi. Routledge, 2017, pp. 11–23.

Tennant, Amanda Berardi. "Rhetorical (In)visibility: How High-Achieving Appalachian Students Navigate their College Experience." *College Composition and Communication*, vol. 73, no. 4, 2022, pp. 10-37. https://doi.org/10.58680/ccc202232014.

———. *Rhetorical (In)visibility: How High-Achieving Appalachian Students Navigate Cultural Identity in and Beyond College*. National Council of Teachers of English, in progress.

Tennant, Amanda Berardi, et al. "From Failure to Inquiry: Three Problem-Solving Strategies for Community Literacy Researchers." *Literacy in Composition Studies*, vol. 10.1, October, 2022. https://doi.org/10.21623/1.10.1.5.

Vatz, R. E. "The Myth of the Rhetorical Situation." *Philosophy and Rhetoric*, vol. 6, 1973, pp. 154–61. https://www.jstor.org/stable/40236848.

Villanueva, Victor. "Blind: Talking about the New Racism." *The Writing Center Journal*, vol. 26, no. 1, 2006, pp. 3–9. https://www.jstor.org/stable/43442234.

Wardle, Elizabeth. "Creative Repurposing for Expansive Learning: Considering 'Problem-Exploring' and 'Answer-Getting' Dispositions in Individuals and Fields." *Composition Forum*, vol. 26, 2012. https://www.compositionforum.com/issue/26/creative-repurposing.php.

Warner, Michael. *Publics and Counterpublics*. Zone Books, 2002

Welch, Nancy. "The Point Is to Change It: Problems and Prospects for Public Rhetors." *College Composition and Communication*, vol. 63, no. 4, 2012, pp. 699–714.

Welch, Nancy, and Tony Scott. *Composition in the Age of Austerity*. Utah State University Press, 2016.

Wertsch, James V. *Voices of the Mind: A Sociocultural Approach to Mediated Action*. Harvard UP, 1991.

West, Cornel. *Keeping Faith: Philosophy and Race in America*. Routledge, 1993.

Wolfe, Joanna. *Team Writing*. Bedford/St. Martin's, 2010.

Yancey, Kathleen Blake. "Introduction." *A Rhetoric of Reflection*, ed. Kathleen Blake Yancey, Utah State UP, 2016, pp. 3–20.

———, editor. *A Rhetoric of Reflection*. Utah State UP, 2016.

Young, Richard E., et al. *Rhetoric: Discovery and Change*. Harcourt, Brace & World, 1970.

Woolley, Anita, and Thomas Malone. "Defend Your Research: What Makes a Team Smarter? More Women." *Harvard Business Review*, June 2011, pp. 32–33.

Index

A
activity 22, 25, 31, 36, 40, 44, 98, 116
assessment 11, 13, 25, 29, 30, 31, 33, 40, 60, 62, 64, 76

C
circulation 50, 51, 52, 53, 55, 56, 61, 72, 79, 97, 121
collaboration 26, 98, 102, 120
community engaged education 6, 18
Community Literacy Center 3, 8, 30, 32, 48, 64, 81, 125, 126
conflict 16, 17, 23, 26, 36, 43, 45, 50, 51, 54, 80, 81, 91, 102, 103, 115, 116, 120, 123, 133
critical incident interviews 27, 30

D
decision makers 5, 56, 68

F
frame 69, 70, 71, 72, 73, 74, 75, 76, 77, 79, 81, 82, 83, 84, 85, 86, 87, 89, 90
frame analysis 50, 77, 78, 80, 84, 117, 119

G
grounded theory 116, 122, 132

I
interpretation 61, 79, 123, 133

L
leadership 33, 44, 101, 105
  adaptive 84, 94

M
mediational tools 36, 55
metacognitive path 20, 78, 116, 126
  metacognitive analysis 84
methods 7, 18, 27, 44

N
negotiated meaning 81, 125, 130

O
outcomes 5, 6, 7, 11, 25, 42, 94
  as transfer 19
  knowledge 98
  measuring 50
  personal 29
  public 47
  unseen 18
  visible 11

R
reflection 7, 23, 34, 37, 40, 78
rhetorical situation 117, 132
rival hypotheses 31, 38, 58, 75, 87, 132
rivaling 31, 32, 39, 55, 63, 105, 108

S
service learning 8, 29
situated knowledge 12, 18, 49, 79

T
think tank 5, 17, 33, 34, 39, 41, 52, 53, 84, 99, 103, 105, 107, 108, 110, 111, 112, 123
transfer 5, 6, 19, 32, 47, 106, 109, 112, 115
transformation 5, 6, 14, 27, 32, 84, 93, 94, 95, 100, 103, 106, 109, 111, 115, 126, 127
  expansive 36, 54

W
working knowledge 6, 40, 45, 93, 98, 99, 100, 102, 104, 105
working theory 80, 81, 83, 85, 86, 87, 116, 122

www.ingramcontent.com/pod-product-compliance
Lightning Source LLC
Chambersburg PA
CBHW060611080526
44585CB00013B/772